KITCHEN
GARDEN
EXPERTS

❖

TWENTY CELEBRATED CHEFS
& THEIR HEAD GARDENERS

❖

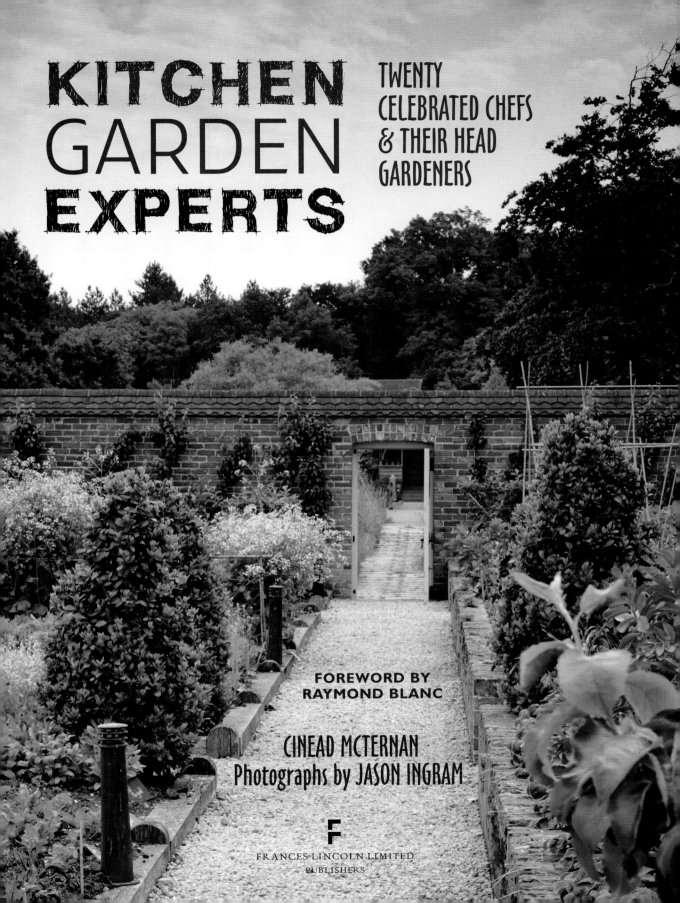

KITCHEN GARDEN EXPERTS

TWENTY CELEBRATED CHEFS & THEIR HEAD GARDENERS

FOREWORD BY
RAYMOND BLANC

CINEAD MCTERNAN
Photographs by JASON INGRAM

F
FRANCES LINCOLN LIMITED
PUBLISHERS

SCOTLAND

GLASGOW

EDINBURGH

12

14

13

NEWCASTLE

3

5

8

YORK

17

ENGLAND

WALES

BIRMINGHAM

1

6

CARDIFF

19

CAMBRIDGE

10

2

20

OXFORD

LONDON

18

11

15

4

16

9

EXETER

7

CONTENTS

Frances Lincoln Ltd
74–77 White Lion Street
London N1 9PF
www.franceslincoln.com

Kitchen Garden Experts
Copyright © Frances Lincoln Ltd 2014
Text copyright © Cinead McTernan 2014
Photographs copyright © Jason Ingram 2014
Map copyright © Frances Lincoln Ltd 2014

First Frances Lincoln edition 2014

A catalogue record for this book is available
from the British Library

ISBN 978-0-7112-3496-3

Printed in China

9 8 7 6 5 4 3 2 1

Illustration acknowledgments
The following illustrations from Shutterstock
were used to create artwork in this book
Cover: background texture © aopsan;
back cover chalkboard © Elena Kalistratova;
back cover carrot and pea illustrations ©
smilewithjul.
Half-title page illustration © Marfa Sobakina
Map: background ©Artindo; food and
cutlery details © Nenilkime; car © Ziven

FOREWORD

By Raymond Blanc

As a child in France I experienced a world in which growing and harvesting vegetables were at the heart of everyday life. Our gardens were used mostly for growing crops rather than flowers, and my own family had a big garden: I would often be sent out to pick fresh produce for Maman Blanc. The garden would help feed the family for the whole year.

I believe it is our responsibility to embrace sustainability and to reconnect with our land – a message I've championed since moving to England more than thirty years ago. By working with the seasons, we can all enjoy superb tastes and textures – inexpensively.

In recent years, consumers have been disempowered and manipulated. Many people no longer fully appreciate how their food is grown, the variety available to them or its seasonality. Now, though, things are changing.

Each aspect of what we do at Le Manoir aux Quat'Saisons is driven by ethical, environmental, seasonal and regional values, whenever possible. What may not have been achievable yesterday is often achievable today. For example, farmers are now reconnecting with their craft, lost through decades of dependency on fertilizers and pesticides. At last, we can find some good-quality produce on our doorstep.

Today, food is being talked about in a new and exciting way, with consumers asking important questions about how it is produced and where it comes from.

My role with The Royal Horticultural Society's 'Edible Britain' campaign – part of the RHS's Britain in Bloom movement – is to help inform and inspire communities about the benefits of using fresh, seasonal produce. As president of Garden Organic, at Le Manoir I have, with my staff, created an extraordinary, new garden for heritage fruit and vegetables, so that we can show the rich variety of produce available in each region of the country.

It is wonderful to see our chefs here in the United Kingdom finally reclaiming their terroir, but it has taken a long time.

The more we can do to change attitudes about such a simple thing as growing fruit and vegetables, the more we can enrich people's plates – and lives.

I hope that the wonderful work of the chefs and growers shown in this book will help more and more people reconnect with the land and encourage them to grow fresh vegetables for themselves, their friends and their families.

Raymond Blanc OBE

INTRODUCTION

We are both growers – we fall into the 'container veg' category – and are both foodies – we have the waistlines to prove it. It was therefore thrilling to meet the chefs and growers featured in this book and to see how the best in the business ensure their productive plots fuel their innovative, award-winning kitchens. Witnessing the chefs' passion for seasonality and provenance was enthralling – they opened our eyes to new ways of using a crop (these chefs want to use *every* part of it – from root to shoot).

When it comes to what can be harvested and eaten, it appears that these chefs have thrown away the rule book – with truly exciting results – and their growers are only too keen to oblige and bring their ideas to the table. This collaboration has pushed the boundaries of growing edible crops and has resulted in the production of high-quality food that is both flavoursome and attractive.

For those of us who 'grow our own' – whether in a kitchen garden, allotment or in containers – it is hugely important to cook with crops that are fresh and in season. Many more of us are choosing to know where our food comes from, as we seek the opportunity to reduce food kilometres where possible. It is also an important environmental consideration that we change how we buy our day-to-day ingredients, that we look to the seasons for inspiration when it comes to home cooking, and that we celebrate local produce and producers. This interest in food goes beyond a feel-good story or a superficial claim to be the new Tom and Barbara from the 1970s' UK television series *The Good Life*: it is also great fun and very satisfying to source good food as well as harvest home-grown fruit and veg.

In the past year we were lucky enough to spend time with some of the most talented growers in the UK, all of whom were unfailingly generous in sharing their horticultural knowledge. After visiting the twenty kitchen gardens described in *Kitchen Garden Experts* and learning the secrets of the growers, we now look at our own veg plot with renewed enthusiasm. We feel confident enough to experiment with varieties and try new techniques. Our 'kitchen garden experts' have elevated growing-your-own to new heights that will appeal to foodies as much as to growers.

Cinead McTernan

Jason Ingram

THE GROVE

Pembrokeshire

The Grove's head gardener, David Butt, has an encyclopedic knowledge of growing vegetables and almost all his sentences include a gardening tip or fact. Gardening is in David's bones, and he has a wonderful knack for relaying information so that it makes complete sense. Unsurprisingly his kitchen garden is immaculate and thriving.

The enthusiasm of The Grove's chef, Duncan Barham, for gardening is as infectious, though he is relatively new to the idea of cooking with home-grown produce. He has quickly become adept at using all parts of a crop – root, stem, leaf and flower. Duncan is passionate about taking simple produce and cooking up something exciting and delectable. His style is a mix of modern British and classical French techniques. Together, David and Duncan make an impressive combination of culinary expertise and horticultural experience, after having both joined The Grove in 2010, when the kitchen garden had been laid out but not yet cultivated.

The Grove's amply stocked, 0.4 hectare/1 acre kitchen garden is managed organically (though not certified as such) by David, with occasional help during the busier spring and autumn months. It includes edible flowers, fruit beds and herbs as well as a polytunnel for more tender plants. The plot provides between 15 per cent of The Grove's winter ingredients and an impressive 75 per cent of their summer ingredients and is testament to traditional techniques: the idea of feeding the soil rather than the plant; the practice of crop rotation; and knowing what does and does not thrive in the clay-silty soil.

There is a lot of rain in this part of Pembrokeshire, and the climate is occasionally damp, so David

OPPOSITE David and Duncan share a passion for growing vegetables.
BELOW The Grove has a beehive near the vegetable garden to help with pollination.

The grower,
David Butt

The chef,
Duncan Barham

cannot grow garlic (which hates having wet feet), and he prefers to grow tomatoes under cover and avoid mass planting potatoes. (*Phytophthora*, or potato blight, is a problem at The Grove, and rather than risk introducing blight in potatoes – which might be passed on to a tomato crop – they plant small numbers of early potatoes, which mature before midsummer, when blight occurs.)

EXOTIC EXPERIMENTS

David likes to grow unusual crops that are generally unavailable or expensive. Oca, a tuber from South America, with its pretty pink roots and delicious citrus flavour, has thrived and provided Duncan with a great novelty for the menu. David also prefers varieties that produce a small harvest over successive weeks rather than huge gluts that might be wasted.

Edible flowers have proved a great success too, both in terms of yield and growth rate, inspiring Duncan to experiment beyond pot marigolds (*Calendula*) and pansies (*Viola* x *wittrockiana*).

It was the new kitchen garden that originally attracted Duncan to The Grove, and it has had a significant impact on the way he designs dishes for the menu. Before The Grove, Duncan had worked near London, where he could source any ingredient from anywhere in the world to be delivered the following day. Now he looks to the garden to see what is ready for the kitchen, which crops are in season, and what is the optimum time to harvest them and capture their best flavour. Duncan loves the idea that, even if he is halfway through a lunch or dinner service, he or any of his chefs can go into the garden to harvest fresh supplies.

While both Duncan and David agree that running a kitchen garden is not a cheaper alternative to buying in fruit, vegetables and herbs, it is the very best way to ensure provenance. Guests can share the magic of this special place, not just by eating the produce but also by taking a tour of the plot, or even harvesting crops themselves if they are staying in one of The Grove's holiday cottages.

BELOW To make some garlic spray, pour 10 litres/2 gallons water into a large container. Then place 400g/14oz garlic granules in a muslin bag (1) and tie it to the inside of the container (2). Leave to infuse. Decant the liquid after 24 hours, retaining the granules, which can last as long as they emit their garlicky scent. To use, dilute 100ml/3½fl oz garlic infusion in 10 litres/2 gallons water in a watering can and apply over the plants (3).

BABY BEETROOT

Beetroot is a popular vegetable with diners at The Grove. To make sure there is a steady supply, David starts beetroot off in mid-winter, sowing it in the polytunnel so that Duncan and his team can start harvesting leaves a few weeks later for salads and garnishes. The root is best eaten when baby-sized (think golf ball) but can be left to mature (until the size of a tennis ball). With the right varieties successively sown, beetroot can be eaten nearly all year round, which is hugely beneficial for a kitchen, as it provides colour and texture on a plate, especially during the 'hungry gap' (which occurs generally in late spring, before summer crops are ripe).

Duncan and David prefer the round varieties of beetroot as they grow nearer the top of the soil so are easier to crop and harvest, while cylindrical ones, being longer, can bleed when being pulled out of the ground; they are also not always successful on clay soil. They select 'Boltardy', 'Bull's Blood' and 'Detroit' varieties for their colourful, cut-and-come-again leaves, which they use like chard. For extra colour they grow 'Golden' (yellow), 'Chioggia' (candy striped) and 'Albina Ice' (white).

TRADITIONAL TECHNIQUES

Beetroot seeds are, horticulturally speaking, multiple fruit, which means there is more than one seed within the coat. David therefore advises sowing them thinly and allowing a clump of seedlings to establish. Harvesting the small ones first allows the remaining beetroot to mature. In dry weather, David also advocates pre-watering the soil drill before sowing, and, if doing this on clay soil, he suggests turning the rose on the watering can face down, so it waters just the base of the drill and not the surrounding soil, which will remain dry and easy to crumble when pulled back over the seeds after sowing.

Once germination has occurred, always ensure the crop is kept moist. If the tops of the beetroot start to look corky, they probably need more water. If 'bolting' occurs, when beetroot flowers and sets seed rather than producing edible roots, it might be worth changing to bolt-resistant varieties of beetroot.

BEETROOT CALENDAR

SOW Sowing traditionally lasts from mid-spring to midsummer, while varieties like 'Boltardy', which resists bolting, can be sown under cloches or in a polytunnel from mid- to late winter; they can also be sown in the open ground in drills from early spring, during a spell of warm dry weather.
CARE Beetroot needs plenty of organic matter and well-drained soil. If space is an issue, this crop is worth growing in a container.
HARVEST Harvest from early summer to mid-autumn, storing late summer-sown varieties over winter.

BEETROOT TEXTURES

INGREDIENTS

SALT-BAKED BEETROOT
1 medium red beetroot
Sprigs of thyme
Salt

BEETROOT COUSCOUS
150ml/¼ pint beetroot juice
4 tsp extra-virgin olive oil
125g/4oz couscous
Maldon sea salt
Freshly ground white pepper

PICKLING LIQUOR
360ml/12fl oz mirin wine
75ml/2½fl oz white wine vinegar
25g/1oz caster sugar
1 star anise
Juice of 1 lemon

PICKLED GOLDEN BEETROOT
1 medium golden beetroot
Salt
Pinch of caster sugar

PICKLED APPLE
1 Granny Smith apple
Pickling liquor

CANDY BEET CRISPS
1 candy-striped beetroot
Icing sugar, for dusting
Maldon sea salt

BEETROOT REDUCTION
250ml/8fl oz beetroot juice

HORSERADISH CRÈME FRAÎCHE
125g/4oz Colman's horseradish sauce
100ml/3½fl oz whipping cream
100ml/3½fl oz crème fraîche
Maldon sea salt
½ leaf of bronze gelatine

The lovely earthy flavour of beetroot can work all year round as either a light addition to spring and summer dishes or as a robust and rich ingredient during autumn and winter. Here Duncan has used it to create a light-textured salad, showcasing the versatility of the humble beetroot. The salt-baked beetroot element of this dish is also a fantastic accompaniment to beef and venison, and the horseradish crème fraîche works brilliantly with fish such as salmon and mackerel.

METHOD

1   **For the salt-baked beetroot**, preheat the oven to 160°C/325°F/gas mark 3. Wash the beetroot well in cold water and trim the stalks and roots. Place in a reasonably tight-fitting, deep saucepan or oven tray. Place the thyme around the beetroot and pack the salt into the remaining space to cover the beetroot. Cook in the oven for 40–60 minutes or until the beetroot is tender when pierced with the tip of a knife. Once cooked, remove from the heat and allow to cool. Remove the beetroot from the salt crust and peel away the outer skin (the salt can be broken down and used again for this process). The beetroot can then be sliced.

2   **For the beetroot couscous**, heat the beetroot juice and olive oil in a saucepan until it begins to simmer. Place the couscous in a mixing bowl and pour over the hot beetroot juice. Give the bowl a gentle shake to combine the ingredients, then cover with clingfilm and allow to stand for 5 minutes. Remove the clingfilm and use a fork to stir the couscous – this will loosen the grains and make it 'fluffy'. Cover the bowl with clingfilm again and stand for another 5 minutes. Stir the couscous with a fork once more and season to taste with the salt and pepper.

3   **For the pickling liquor**, combine all the ingredients for the pickling liquor in a saucepan and warm gently until the sugar dissolves completely.

4   **For the pickled golden beetroot**, place the golden beetroot in a saucepan and cover with water, add the salt and sugar and gently simmer until the beetroot is tender. Discard the cooking water and allow to cool sufficiently for the skins to be peeled away. While the beetroot and pickling liquor are still warm, place in a

clean jar so the beetroot is completely covered by the liquor (reserve a small amount of the liquor for the pickled apple). Allow at least 24 hours for the beetroot to pickle. Once pickled, slice or dice the beetroot; it can be stored in the refrigerator for two weeks or so.

5   **For the pickled apple**, finely slice the apple on a mandolin, taking care not to slice through the core. While it is still warm, pour a small amount of pickling liquor over the apple slices and allow to steep for a few hours before using.

6   **For the candy beet crisps**, finely slice the beetroot from top to bottom using an electric slicer or mandolin. With a round cutter, cut out the centre of each slice and discard the outer rings. Lay the slices flat on a nonstick baking sheet and dust with the icing sugar and a light sprinkling of crushed sea salt. Place in a dehydrator or an oven set at 110°C/225°F/gas mark ¼ until the slices become crisp. Store in a dry airtight container until required.

7   **For the beetroot reduction**, gently simmer the beetroot juice in a saucepan over a low heat until the liquid has a slightly sticky, syrupy consistency. Allow the syrup to cool.

8   **For the horseradish crème fraîche**, blend the horseradish sauce and 85ml/3fl oz of the cream in a blender until smooth. Pass the mixture through a fine sieve into a mixing bowl, to remove any of the fibrous pieces of horseradish. Add the crème fraîche and a pinch of salt to the bowl and stir in well. Warm the remaining cream in a small saucepan. Soften the gelatine in cold water, squeeze out any excess water and add to the warm cream; stir until dissolved. Pour the gelatine mix into the mixing bowl containing the horseradish cream

and combine well. Place in the refrigerator and allow to set.

9   **To assemble the dish**, lay slices of salt-baked beetroot on a plate. Spoon on some couscous and arrange the pickled golden beetroot, pickled apple and candy beet crisps on top. Use a pastry brush to paint the beetroot reduction on the plate. Serve with the horseradish crème fraîche.

TENDER RHUBARB

David grows three varieties of rhubarb – 'Victoria', 'Timperley' and 'Champagne'. Succulent young rhubarb is a real treat early in the season so he forces some of these plants. To do this, David prefers the traditional Victorian method of lifting the crowns when frost is likely, to kick-start them into growth, rather than covering the crowns so that the stems are grown in darkness, thereby preventing chlorophyll from stiffening them. His method brings forward the harvest time by around ten days. Although rhubarb is traditionally left to grow in the same spot, it can be moved when dormant in winter. David successfully transplanted his rhubarb crowns from the main beds to the fruit beds last winter, where he placed them in a uniform line, making them more accessible for general maintenance. He mulches around the rhubarb plants with garden compost and occasionally applies an additional feed of general fertilizer throughout the season. The worst thing for rhubarb is being waterlogged in winter: it performs best in an open, free-draining spot. Watch out for crown rot as a result of waterborne fungi or bacteria, and cut away affected areas. Rhubarb can also flourish in large containers if well watered and fed.

RHUBARB CALENDAR

SOW Sow rhubarb from seed in late winter (with bottom heat) or direct sow in early spring.
PLANT You can also start with a clump of rhubarb roots called a crown, planted in autumn or spring, after having added plenty of well-rotted manure to the plot. Plant so just the tip of the crown can be seen above the soil.
HARVEST Some varieties such as 'Glaskin's Perpetual' can be cropped lightly after one season, but it is best to allow the plant to bulk up before harvesting stems.

DAVID & DUNCAN'S
KITCHEN GARDEN SECRETS

- **Micro-leaves**: Grow micro-leaves in the soil rather than a container because they are easier to keep well watered. In the reduced amounts of soil available in a container plants have less water available in reserve and often suffer setbacks due to over- and underwatering.

- **Garlic spray**: David uses garlic spray (see page 12) as preventative and tonic. He finds that it reduces infestations of carrot fly and caterpillars as well as enhances plant health. He always uses a watering can to apply the garlic spray, and does not water it on to the plants in direct sunlight. When the granules are spent, he scatters them on to the soil.

- **Totally edible**: Choose plants of which you can eat all the parts: for example, with a radish you can use the roots, leaves, flowers and pods; with broccoli, the floret, flowers and stems are edible; with celeriac you can eat the roots and leaves. Think of vegetables in the way you think of meat – eating from head to tail.

- **Good neighbours**: Grow sacrificial crops to lure pests away from your main crop. Companion planting is also worth a try: for example, mustards are said to be helpful in the battle against eelworm in potato beds – as are nasturtium in a brassica plot, and marigolds among carrots.

POACHED RHUBARB WITH BUTTERMILK PUDDING, HONEYCOMB & GINGER WINE

SERVES 2

INGREDIENTS

BUTTERMILK PUDDING
150ml/¼ pint whipping cream
65g/2oz caster sugar
1¾ leaves of gelatine
300ml/½ pint buttermilk
Juice of 1 lemon

POACHED RHUBARB
3 sticks of rhubarb
200ml/⅓ pint sweet white wine
200g/7oz caster sugar
50ml/2fl oz beetroot juice

RHUBARB CRISP
100g/3½oz water
100g/3½oz caster sugar
2 drops of red food colouring
1 stick of rhubarb

RHUBARB SORBET
250g/9oz poached rhubarb skins
100ml/3½fl oz rhubarb syrup
40ml/1½fl oz inverted sugar syrup
1 leaf of gelatine

HONEYCOMB
110g/4oz caster sugar
55ml/2fl oz honey
40ml/1½fl oz liquid glucose
4 tsp water
1 tsp sodium bicarbonate

GINGER WINE FLUID GEL
40g/1½oz caster sugar
125ml/4fl oz Stone's ginger wine
⅓ tsp agar agar powder
Juice of ½ a lemon

TO DECORATE
Wild wood sorrel leaves

Early-season rhubarb signifies the start of spring and at The Grove we grow three heritage varieties, 'Victoria', 'Timperley' and 'Champagne', which generally see us through until the end of summer. Its natural sweet 'n' sour flavour makes it perfect for sweet and savoury dishes, and if Duncan has a lot left at the end of the season he uses it for chutneys and preserves. For this recipe his preference would be to use the 'Champagne' variety of rhubarb – its delicate crisp flavour and vivid pink colour are perfect. However any rhubarb variety can be used, but add a little extra sugar if it is particularly sour.

METHOD

1 **For the buttermilk pudding**, in a small saucepan, warm 50ml/2fl oz of the cream with the sugar until the sugar dissolves. Soften the gelatine in cold water, squeeze out any excess water and add to the warm cream and sugar. Stir until the gelatine is completely dissolved. Place the buttermilk into a mixing bowl, add the cream mixture and combine well. Lightly whip the rest of the cream to the ribbon stage and fold it into the buttermilk. Fold in the lemon juice. Pour into lightly greased moulds and refrigerate until set.

2 **For the poached rhubarb**, using a vegetable peeler, peel the outer red skin from the rhubarb. Retain the skin and the stalks. In a saucepan, combine the wine, sugar and rhubarb skins. Bring to the boil and remove from the heat. Allow to cool, then pass the mixture through a fine sieve. Retain the skins and the syrup for poaching and to make the sorbet. Cut the peeled rhubarb into pieces about 3cm/1¼in long and place in a vacuum pouch along with 100ml/3½fl oz syrup. Vacuum and seal the pouch, then cook in a water bath at 60°C/140°F for 12–15 minutes or until the rhubarb is soft to the touch. Allow to cool then remove from the bag. Retain the rhubarb pieces and the syrup.

3 **For the rhubarb crisp**, make a stock syrup by combining the water and sugar in a saucepan and bring to the boil until the sugar has dissolved. Add the food colouring, mix well and allow to cool slightly. Peel the outer skin from the rhubarb stalk and, using a vegetable peeler, remove even strips of rhubarb from the top of the stalk to the bottom. Dip the strips of rhubarb in the stock syrup. Drain off any excess syrup and lay the strips flat and straight on a baking sheet lined with a silicone baking mat. Place the rhubarb strips in a dehydrator, or a very low oven (65°C/150°F/gas mark ¼) with the door slightly ajar, until they are completely dry. Remove the strips from the silicone mat and store until required in an airtight container.

4 **For the rhubarb sorbet**, in a blender, purée the poached rhubarb skins until smooth, then pass through a fine sieve to remove any stringy fibres. Gently warm the rhubarb syrup and inverted sugar syrup in a saucepan, then add the rhubarb purée. Soften the gelatine in cold water, squeeze out any excess water and add to the warm mixture to dissolve the gelatine. Allow this mixture to cool and churn it in an ice cream machine until it forms a sorbet. Remove from the ice cream machine and keep in a freezer until needed.

5 **For the honeycomb**, place all the ingredients, except the sodium bicarbonate, in a large saucepan and cook over a high heat until the mixture turns a light caramel colour. Remove from the heat and add the sodium bicarbonate to the pan and quickly whisk into the mixture for 10–15 seconds until the mixture achieves a honeycomb colour. Using a spatula, carefully pour the honeycomb from the pan on to a baking sheet lined with greaseproof paper and allow to cool. The honeycomb can be broken or chopped into smaller pieces and kept for up to a week in an airtight container.

6 **For the ginger wine fluid gel**, in a small saucepan, dissolve the sugar into half of the ginger wine. Add the agar agar to the saucepan and mix in well, bring to the boil and continue to stir well for 1–2 minutes until the agar agar has dissolved. Remove the pan from the heat and add the rest of the ginger wine and the lemon juice and combine well. Pour the mixture into a container and refrigerate until the jelly has set firm. Place the jelly in a blender and blitz it at high speed until the mixture is a smooth purée. It can then be transferred to a squeezy bottle to serve.

6 **To serve**, arrange the rhubarb pieces and a crisp rhubarb on a plate, On them, scatter some of the chopped honeycomb, followed by the buttermilk pudding and rhubarb sorbet. Squeeze a few drops of the ginger wine fluid gel around the dish and finish with a few wild wood sorrel leaves.

2

THE ETHICUREAN

Somerset

Mark Cox's journey from hobby grower to market gardener began in 2001 in a walled garden in north Somerset. Very few can claim to have had such magical surroundings in which to try their hand at growing crops for the first time – these days securing an allotment plot can take you a few years but finding an unused walled garden is very difficult. Good fortune was on his side again in 2003, when he had proved to be a successful grower and needed to expand his business. Remarkably he stumbled on Barley Wood Walled Garden, in the nearby village of Wrington. Now the produce from his kitchen gardens supplies farmers' markets, veg box customers and The Ethicurean – a beautiful, award-winning restaurant in the Victorian glasshouses of Barley Wood Walled Garden.

Unsurprisingly the magical location and connection with a kitchen garden was the reason The Ethicurean team (chefs and brothers Iain and Matthew Pennington, mixologist Jack Adair-Bevan and front-of-house Paûla Zarate) chose to open a restaurant there. They admit to rarely leaving the beautiful walled garden, which is an absolute paradise. Iain and Matthew favour seasonal local produce above all else, and it determines what is featured on their daily changing menu.

PERFECT COMPANIONS

The relationship between chefs and grower at Barley Wood is exciting: the Pennington brothers' food is modern and based around the best crop of the day. Mark loves to grow and experiment, which provides the chefs with an intriguing larder. Mark has tried quinoa, a cereal crop grown for its seed, and achocha, an unusual vegetable from South America that is eaten raw and tastes like green peppers. One of Mark's favourite discoveries is electric daisies (*Acmella oleracea*). It has a fiery little flower that leaves your tongue tingling as if you have licked a 9-volt battery, but it has yet to receive approval from customers of The Ethicurean.

OPPOSITE The view from Barley Wood Walled Garden is across Wrington Vale and the Mendip Hills in Somerset.

The grower,
Mark Cox

The chef,
Iain Pennington

The chef,
Matthew Pennington

The mixologist,
Jack Adair-Bevan

Iain, Matthew and Mark see each other almost daily so have plenty of opportunity to talk about what is ready to harvest now or in the next few weeks, and of any new varieties to try. Mark's veg box customers are a great source of information too. A recent suggestion from an Italian customer was cima di rapa, a form of broccoli that is new to many growers in the UK. Sown successively for winter and early spring harvests, it produces delicious large succulent leaves.

Both chefs and gardener prefer heritage varieties, finding them more flavoursome. Mark would rather contend with pests and diseases than grow hybrid, disease-resistant varieties, which he believes to be less tasty. There are exceptions to this, such as tomatoes, which pose an interesting dilemma: soft-skinned heritage varieties have a far superior taste, but they are delicate and do not travel well, and this is a problem for the farmers' markets and veg boxes. Hybrids have tougher skins and are therefore more commercial. Although, if home-grown, hybrids will still beat the watery supermarket versions. Mark's solution is to grow tomatoes in two polytunnels, one filled with heritage varieties such as the Russian black beefsteak 'Paul Robeson', and the other planted with hybrids such as 'Gardener's Delight'.

SALAD DAYS

During the summer The Ethicurean restaurant uses 1kg/2lb 3oz salad leaves every day. To ensure plenty of variety and flavour for the kitchen, Mark grows mixed salad collections such as 'Braising', which includes red and green mustard, kale, tatsoi and hon tsai tai and French blend, with rocket, curled chervil, red Batavia lettuce and chicory 'Rossa di Verona'. Interestingly Mark finds the best salad leaves are produced during the winter, when there are virtually no pests. This is also his favourite time of year in the plot, and he agrees with growing guru Joy Larkcom's philosophy that there need not be a hungry gap. Careful planning ensures a steady stream of produce.

For Mark, the connection with The Ethicurean makes his experience as a grower more enriching and wholesome, especially as Barley Wood Walled Garden is open to the public and restaurant visitors, who can wander around at leisure.

BELOW LEFT Matthew, Mark and Iain check if the runner beans are yet ready to harvest.
BELOW RIGHT Radish seed pods are a welcome addition to The Ethicurean's seasonal menu.

CRUNCHY RADISHES

Radishes are useful in any garden as they are quick to germinate and produce a crop, and you can eat all its parts at different times of year – from root to shoot, flower and seed pod. Mark grows 'French Breakfast', 'Pink Beauty', 'White Beauty' and 'Rat's Tail' (the last is cultivated for its crisp crunchy seed pods rather than its root). He sows early in the season to avoid problems with flea beetle in early summer. He also covers the crop with fleece to deter this pest, which marks tender young leaves with pitted holes and makes them unusable in the kitchen. Mark also sows radishes between rows of garlic and lettuce.

RADISH CALENDAR

SOW Direct sow in drills in open ground, spacing one seed every 2.5cm/1in. For early crops, cover with a cloche or horticultural fleece to warm the soil.

CARE Mark prefers the seeds to find a water supply by sending out long roots, so he does not pre-water the drills before sowing. As a result of adding organic matter, the soil is a crumbly loam in which radishes thrive.

HARVEST Summer radish varieties should be harvested when they are small. However winter radishes are more robust and can remain in the soil until required, or be lifted in late autumn and stored in a cool dry place.

TRADITIONAL BROCCOLI

Another robust winter crop at Barley Wood is sprouting broccoli, which is hardy enough to overwinter and is ready for harvest by the end of winter. Mark also experiments with new varieties such as broccoli 'Brakali Apollo', a Chinese variety that bears soft tender stems and flower buds with a delicious and distinctive flavour. Being quick growing, its stems are ready to harvest two to three months after sowing. In addition he grows calabrese as a summer crop, which he sows successionally. Broccoli requires well-drained soil without extra organic matter, as this can promote unwanted soft leafy growth. Mark waters regularly and uses netting to protect the plants from birds.

BROCCOLI CALENDAR

SOW For calabrese, single-head broccoli types, choose a sunny sheltered spot and direct sow in open ground. Thin seedlings to 30cm/12in apart, and keep them well watered. For sprouting and Chinese varieties, direct sow in mid- or late spring in a spot that can be left undisturbed.

CARE Use horticultural fleece to protect plants from pigeons. To encourage plenty of tasty and tender side shoots that can be cropped over a long period, remove each central head when it appears.

HARVEST Crop calabrese in late summer or early autumn. Sprouting and Chinese varieties will not be ready for harvesting until late winter or early spring. Eat the broccoli flowers once the plant starts to bolt.

RADISH ROOTS & SEED PODS, BUTTERMILK SNOW & LOVAGE SALT

SERVES 2

Mark has shown us that radishes grown through warm sunny times taste hotter, because they develop more isothiocyanate compounds; these are also found in mustards. In this recipe the hot radishes are given a cooling partner in the form of a buttermilk snow. Radish and salt has long been considered a great duo, and the addition of our favourite herb, lovage, enhances them even more. By sowing radishes a couple of weeks apart, we can use seed pods of bolted radish while also have tender roots of new growth at the same time. The lactofermentation of root vegetables is a technique that allows us to save produce for winter, and in this case we have used purple carrots. We have reduced the normal salt level in the carrot juice so as to have a delicious liquid by-product that can be taken as a healthy tonic drink – good for the gut.

INGREDIENTS

CARROT JUICE
150g/5oz purple carrots or beetroot, peeled and
   sliced into 4cm/1½in pieces
500ml/17½fl oz mineral water
1 tsp salt
25g/¾oz whey (see Labneh recipe, page 28)

BUTTERMILK SNOW
500ml/17½fl oz cultured buttermilk
1 tbsp honey or maple syrup

LOVAGE SALT
200g/7oz salt, frozen
Bunch of fresh lovage leaves, harvested on a dry
   warm day

TO SERVE
3 radishes, including leaves, washed and sliced
Handful of radish seed pods

LOVAGE

Lovage (*Levisticum officinale*) is easy to grow, although it does need a cold snap to trigger germination so is best sown in autumn. Plant out in spring in a well-prepared, shady or sunny spot that has had plenty of organic matter added to the soil. Clip the plant in summer to ensure tender young leaves. After a few years divide in spring, to bulk up your stocks. Harvest seeds when they are nearly ripe, then dry them for using in biscuits, bread and soups.

METHOD

1   **For the lactofermented carrot juice**, place the carrot or beetroot pieces in a sterilized, 1-litre/1¾-pint kilner jar. Add the mineral water, salt and whey. Keep at about 20°C/68°F for 2–3 days. Open the jar every day to relieve the pressure that builds inside it; also taste the liquid – it will have become mildly acidic and similar to yogurt in taste. **Then** refrigerate for 4 days to deepen the colour of the liquid and allow it to thicken slightly. Thereafter remove the carrot or beetroot pieces, which can be eaten or saved for a second preparation if so desired. If you plan on keeping the carrot juice for longer than a month, test its pH, which should be lower than 3.9.

2   **For the buttermilk snow**, mix the buttermilk and syrup well together. Freeze in a lidded airtight container.

3   **For the lovage salt**, blend the ingredients together until the herb is well combined. Pass through a sieve to remove any remaining fibres and then freeze the mix in a sealed container until needed. This method works well when preserving many types of summer herbs.

4   **To serve**, assemble the dish on frozen plates to allow the melting buttermilk snow to be enjoyed a little longer. Scrape the frozen buttermilk block over and over with fork prongs to create the snow. Add to the frozen plates with the radish slices, seed pods and 1 tbsp carrot juice. Garnish the dish with the bright green lovage salt and enjoy as soon as possible.

DUCK FLIP

SERVES 1

INGREDIENTS

HONEY SYRUP
250g/9oz honey
250ml/9fl oz water

TO SERVE
Handful of lovage leaves
50ml/2fl oz three-year-old Somerset cider brandy
1 duck's egg yolk
6 drops of lactofermented carrot juice
    (see page 25).

The drinks at The Ethicurean are founded on a sense of place. This is the idea of having a connection with the native land, its history and the community who grow food locally. Iain and Matthew like to connect their dishes and drinks, and so pass back and forth ingredients between the kitchen and bar. In this recipe they incorporated a small amount of the liquid from the lactofermented carrot juice recipe (see page 25). Mark grows lovage in the garden and it is added to this drink by the handful. The savoury flavour of lovage is a triumph when combined with Julian Temperley's heady, three-year-old Somerset cider brandy.

METHOD

1   **For the honey syrup**, combine the honey and water in a medium-sized saucepan. Place on a medium–high heat and bring to a simmer. Stir to ensure all the honey has dissolved before taking the saucepan off the heat. The syrup can be stored in a clean container for a week in the refrigerator.

2   **To serve**, infuse half of the lovage leaves in the brandy for 5 minutes. (We use a small glass teapot but any container will suffice.)

3   Add the egg yolk to a cocktail shaker along with 2 tsp honey syrup, the lovage-infused brandy and the remaining lovage leaves. Shake these ingredients together before adding ice cubes and shaking again. A really good hard shake is necessary to introduce air and to chill the drink quickly.

4   Strain the liquid with a sieve into a chilled coupe before pipetting the lactofermented carrot juice on to the surface of the drink. Drink immediately with the Radish Roots & Seed Pods dish (see page 25).

MARK, IAIN & MATTHEW'S
KITCHEN GARDEN SECRETS

- **Quick crops**: Radishes are best grown as a catch crop, in-between slow-growing vegetables. They germinate in a matter of days and mature in weeks, so the radishes will have been harvested before crops such as peas and potatoes fully occupy their ground. Another use for radishes, because of their rapid growth, is to indicate where slow-germinating parsnips have been sown. The line of radishes will mark the spot well, so you can avoid inadvertently hoeing or planting over the rows of parsnip seeds.
- **Decoy plants**: Nasturtiums will lure cabbage white butterflies away from broccoli, while mint helps to repel flea beetles.
- **Source of inspiration**: Joy Larkcom's book, *Grow Your Own Vegetables*, is Mark's bible, and he encourages anyone who is interested in growing their own to follow Joy's advice. Most of the Oriental leaves that we grow today – such as mizuna and mibuna – were pioneered by Joy.
- **Belt and braces**: Mark finds it helpful to plant extra bean plants in the final position as a safety net in case there is a cold snap or windy weather that damages the weaker plants.

THE ETHICUREAN
BARLEY WOOD WALLED GARDEN
TELEPHONE: 01934 863713

VEG FOR SALE

GREY MULLET, BROCCOLINI & PICKLED NASTURTIUM SEEDS

SERVES 2

Broccolini is a hybrid of sprouting broccoli and Chinese Kai-lan broccoli. It has long tender stems and is also know as aspabroc because of its asparagus-like qualities. In this recipe the broccolini flavour is given an extra lift as it has been combined with salted, dried roe of grey mullet, Ancho chilli flakes and Asian-origin, fermented black garlic. The robust brined fillet of fried grey mullet is rich enough to pair with these dominant flavours. When picked fresh from the walled garden, the broccolini is sweet and without woodiness. It is a marvellous vegetable staple here at The Ethicurean.

INGREDIENTS

300g/10oz grey mullet fillet
Rapeseed or groundnut oil
Fine sea salt
200g/7oz broccolini

DRIED MULLET ROES
2 grey mullet roes
500ml/17^1/$_2$fl oz coarse sea salt

BRINE
1 litre/1^3/$_4$ pints water
40g/1^1/$_2$oz natural sea salt
1 tsp fennel seeds
1 tsp aniseed

LABNEH
1 tsp fine natural sea salt
450ml/^{3}/$_4$ pint organic live yogurt

PICKLED NASTURTIUM SEEDS
As many nasturtium seeds as you
    can gather
Fine sea salt
6%+ acidity vintage cider vinegar

FERMENTED BLACK
GARLIC CRISP
2 fermented black garlic cloves

TO GARNISH
Plum rich Ancho chilli flakes
Nasturtium flowers

METHOD

1 **For the dried mullet roes**, add a thick layer of kitchen paper to the base of a non-reactive roasting tray or oven dish, and lay the roe on top. Cover the roe in coarse sea salt, coating completely. Place a lid on top, or cover with a tea towel. Leave somewhere cool for a day or two, for the salt to start removing the moisture from the roe. After this time it is likely that some of salt will have dissolved. Remove the roe from the tray, discard the kitchen paper and replace with new paper. Lay the roe on the paper and cover with more sea salt. Repeat this process until all the moisture has been removed from the roe. This will be apparent when the salt remains completely dry after a day of being in contact with the roe. This can take 4 or more repetitions – making sure all moisture is removed is paramount. When all moisture has been removed, brush off any salt crystals and hang the dried roe somewhere cool and dry for 1 month.

2 **For the brine**, place the water and salt in a medium-sized saucepan and bring to the boil over a moderate heat. Immediately remove from the heat, add the spices and cover with a lid. Allow to rest for 15 minutes, to infuse, before straining into a large tray to cool. Once at room temperature, refrigerate until completely cold.

3 **For the labneh**, blanch a large piece of muslin cloth in boiling water. Drain off the hot water and allow the cloth to cool. Add the salt to the yogurt and stir through until combined. Line a sieve or colander with two layers of the cooled cloth and place over a suitably sized container. Pour the salted yogurt into the lined sieve. Refrigerate the resulting whey overnight. Also use the whey as a starter for the lactofermented carrot element in the Radish Roots & Seed Pods recipe (see page 25).

4 **For the pickled nasturtium seeds**, cover the nasturtium seeds with a generous dusting of salt and leave for 3–4 hours to remove some moisture. Rinse the seeds, then add them to a sterilized jar and cover with the cider vinegar.

Refrigerate and keep for up to six months.

5 **For the fermented black garlic crisp**, preheat the oven to 150°C/300°F/gas mark 2. Roll the garlic cloves thinly between two sheets of nonstick baking paper. Bake for 20–30 minutes. Allow to cool before peeling from the baking paper.

6 **To assemble the dish**, submerge the grey mullet completely in the cold brine. Place in the refrigerator for 30 minutes. Remove from the refrigerator once the time has elapsed, drain the liquid and gently wash the fillets under a running tap. Pat dry on a tea towel. Stir crumbled dried mullet roe into 2 tbsp labneh, to taste, and mix until well combined.

7 Heat a nonstick frying pan over a moderate heat until hot. Lightly brush the skins of the mullet with rapeseed or groundnut oil, and season with fine sea salt. Place the fillets skin-side down in the hot pan and cook for 3–5 minutes, depending on the thickness of the fillets and heat of the burner. The skin should be golden and the bottom half of the fish cooked through. Flip the fish skin-side up and cook it for no more than 1 minute. Place the fish on a warm plate and rest for 1 minute.

8 Blanch the broccolini for 2–3 minutes in salted boiling water. Drain on kitchen paper before serving with a dusting of the chilli flakes. Serve on warmed plates with the remaining accompaniments and nasturtium flowers to garnish.

3

THE GEORGE & DRAGON

Cumbria

Colin Myers has gardened at Askham Hall on the Lowther Estate in the Lake District since 2004. These days the fruit, vegetables and herbs he grows in the 0.2-hectare/½-acre kitchen garden supply the Askham Hall's café and the estate's eighteenth-century coaching inn, The George & Dragon, which is just a few kilometres away in the village of Clifton. But the land has not always been used in this way.

In the early years the plot provided the staple crops for the Lowther family, who lived in the Hall: potatoes, cabbages, onions – that is, as Colin describes them, the traditional bulky crops. However plans to transform Askham Hall into a boutique hotel with a garden café and to restore The George & Dragon had exciting implications. Colin was given a brief to redesign the productive plot and experiment with different varieties so it could supply both the hotel and pub's kitchens with fresh seasonal produce.

After more than ten years of good management by Colin and his predecessors the soil is a wonderful crumbly loam that can grow almost anything. However the garden faces north and is sheltered by laurel hedging, while the imposing Hall blocks the sun and casts long shadows over the plot. The growing season therefore starts late and finishes early. To ensure good germination rates for sowing outside in these testing conditions Colin has learned to read the seasons, patiently waiting for temperatures to rise and the soil to warm up rather than blithely sowing in the month suggested on the seed packet. According to him it is a bit like the hare and the tortoise – the crops are the tortoise and eventually do catch up at harvest time, even if they are slow to get going. In an unpredictable climate it is a useful approach to adopt.

COMING IN FROM THE COLD

The polytunnel is a vital addition to the garden and, even though it is unheated and the benefits are limited, it allows Colin to cheat the shorter season a little. He makes a first sowing of beetroot in mid-winter and starts salads off in late winter, sowing more every couple of weeks for a continuous supply. Tomato, aubergine, chilli and pepper follow – all these plants benefiting from the extra shelter and warmth under cover and providing crops throughout summer.

Prior to the hotel and pub reopening, consultant chef Stephen Doherty was appointed to oversee their individual menus and ensure both kitchens made the most of the estate's 800-year-old tradition of producing the highest-quality meat and vegetables. Stephen is classically trained and worked with celebrated chefs such as Alain Chapel at his restaurant in Mionnay and the Roux brothers at Le Gavroche in London, where he was head chef for five years. His passion for quality and food provenance is shared by all the team at The George & Dragon and Askham Hall.

The grower,
Colin Myers

The chef,
Stephen Doherty

OPPOSITE Colin harvests the delicate courgette flowers first thing in the morning.

When Stephen moved to The George & Dragon, Colin had already begun redesigning the garden at the Hall and had started experimenting with crops. He was delighted to find his plans fitted with Stephen's vision for a range of home-grown produce that could feature on both menus. The large herb bed, placed in the centre of the plot, includes different varieties of thyme, sage and mint, as well as Stephen's selection of edible flowers such as nasturtium, borage and lemon verbena. The remaining raised beds are filled with a mixture of traditional crops: legumes, brassicas, roots and onions. Most of these are harvested as baby vegetables for the kitchen. For Stephen this is when they have optimum flavour, are sweet and tender and are expensive to buy from outside suppliers. Colin grows other valuable but simple crops in the polytunnel, such as baby salad leaves. They are highly prized by the chefs in both kitchens and appear on nearly every plate as a garnish. Raised beds are filled with cut-and-come-again salads – mizuna, mibuna and giant red mustard – in pretty rows of alternating colour and leaf texture.

LEADING THE WAY

Colin is an imaginative gardener and the kitchen garden is full of ideas that visitors can adopt in their own gardens. He has designed 1.25-m/4-ft square beds, each with a central wooden wigwam, for runner and French beans. The beds are small enough to suit most gardens, and they demonstrate how an attractive feature can have a practical purpose. His removable raised-bed cloches are another feat of ingenuity as they cleverly use recycled materials from around the garden: wood offcuts create the main frames, and old plastic tubes form arches to secure the chicken wire. The cloches are light and easy to lift on and off the beds, and they protect seedlings and crops from birds and pests as and when they are required.

Stephen encourages his chefs to include daily specials on the menu to tie in with what is ready in the garden. Each morning Colin harvests his produce, working to the chefs' lists and adding in one or two unexpected crops. Mid-lunch phone calls from the pub occasionally request Colin to bring more salad leaves – perhaps a couple of raised beds in the pub's garden might be a thought?

COURGETTE CALENDAR

SOW Colin sows from early to late spring in pots and grows on the seedlings in the polytunnel.
CARE When the first pair of true leaves appears, he hardens off each plant and transplants it into open ground in late spring. He keeps an eye out for any slugs the birds might have missed, and he also waters the plants regularly, ensuring their roots get a good drink.
HARVEST Cut the courgette and flower together when flowers are in full bloom.

COURGETTES

Colin grows a range of courgettes: 'Romanesco' for its large flowers and tasty flesh, which never becomes watery; the reliable cropper 'Zucchini'; and the prolific, bright yellow 'Atena', with its mellow flavour.

Rather than giving them a weekly feed, Colin prefers to feed the soil outside the growing season. For this he uses green manures such as winter field bean (*Vicia faba*). He sows this in autumn and digs it into the soil in spring, so it provides the plants with nutrients from the start. Colin worries that too much plant food can increase the levels of salt in the soil, so he applies extra feed only occasionally.

The courgettes rarely make it into the kitchen as mature fruit; rather they are harvested when immature with their bright, large yellow flowers attached. Colin simply cuts them at the base when the flower is open. This not only provides a crop for the kitchen but also spurs the plant to produce more flowers and fruits over a longer period.

BABY COURGETTES WITH A GARDEN HERB MAYO

SERVES 4

Courgette flowers conjour up memories of summers and the short season of these delicate flowers, lightly battered and fried in olive oil with garlic reminds Stephen of eating these with friends in Italy.

METHOD

1   Preheat the fryer to 180°C/350°F/gas mark 4 and the oven to the same temperature. Remove the courgette flowers from their stems. Slice the baby courgettes into quarters like a fan, keeping the top intact. In a bowl, whisk together flour with a pinch of salt and turmeric and slowly add the beer until you have got a smooth batter. Allow to rest for 5–10 minutes.

2   Mix together the chilli, garlic, garden herbs, lemon juice and a pinch of salt with the mayonnaise. Lightly dust the baby courgettes in some flour. Dip and coat in the batter and deep-fry in sunflower oil until golden and crispy. Remove from the fryer and drain on a metal tray lined with kitchen paper. Keep the fried baby courgettes hot in the oven.

3   Repeat the battering and deep-frying process with the courgette flowers. Remove the courgettes from the oven and sprinkle the flowers with a few Maldon sea salt flakes.

4   Serve on a colourful plate or board with the mayonnaise on the side. Extra lemon slices may be served to squeeze on top.

INGREDIENTS

12 baby courgettes and flowers
200g/7oz self-raising flour
Maldon sea salt
Turmeric, to taste
150ml/¼ pint light Cumbrian beer – pale ale is good
½ tsp diced red chilli
Knife tip of chopped garlic
2 tsp chopped garden herbs
Lemon juice, to taste
Heaped tsp mayonnaise
Sunflower oil

COLIN & STEPHEN'S
KITCHEN GARDEN SECRETS

- **Optimum time to sow**: Wait until weed seeds start to germinate before sowing seeds outside.
- **Water temperature**: Tepid water is best when watering seedlings in a polytunnel or greenhouse. Never use very cold water.
- **Beetroot clumps**: Sow beetroot in large modular trays, four seeds to a cell. Plant out whole clumps when roots show at the bottom of the cells. Colin finds this way of sowing aids germination and provides a crop of baby-sized beetroot at the start of the season. A few larger roots are left in the ground to mature.
- **Tomatoes in autumn**: Pinch out the tips of polytunnel-grown tomatoes in early autumn, to encourage the fruits to ripen.
- **Harvesting herbs**: Make sure you pick herbs frequently to maintain them in optimum condition. Also trim them regularly to ensure plants stay fresh and healthy.

LEMON VERBENA

Stephen uses lemon verbena (*Aloysia citrodora*) to garnish dishes, both savoury and sweet. This fast-growing herb originates from South America, so it prefers warm indoor conditions. Stephen grows lemon verbena in a corner of the polytunnel, where it will shed some of its leaves in winter, but produce new growth once the weather warms up. If you want to plant this herb outdoors, site it at the foot of a sunny wall in poor, free-draining soil. In such a situation you will get a great crop in the first year but might need to replace the plant in the next one. Harvest lemon verbena leaves little and often and use them at once. You can also dry them, so they retain their zingy flavour. Unlike other flowering herbs, you can keep harvesting lemon verbena leaves while the plant is in flower; you can pick the small, pale-coloured flowers too.

EARLY GOOSEBERRIES

Gooseberries are great for any kitchen. They provide the year's first under-ripe soft fruits in early summer – their tartness being excellent in savoury dishes and pies. By midsummer the fruits are riper and sweeter. Colin's gooseberry bushes are in a large fruit cage situated in front of Askham Hall's café and pizza oven. As they are so visible to the public, he makes sure that his plants always look their best. However the reality is that these ten-year-old bushes, which have cropped well over the years, thanks to a regular winter prune to maintain an open-goblet shape, are coming to the end of their productive lives.

Gooseberry bushes can cope with most soil types and can be trained as cordons or be grown in containers. In spring Colin keeps a watchful eye for signs of gooseberry sawfly: if left unchecked this caterpillar-like larvae will reduce a bush to bare stems. The most organic approach to controlling them is to check the undersides of leaves and the centre of each bush, picking off larvae. However the sawfly can lay eggs three times a year, so once you spot it keep checking throughout summer.

LEMON VERBENA CALENDAR

PROPAGATE As an insurance or to bulk up your stocks of this herb with its lemon-sherbet-flavoured leaves, propagate it by taking softwood cuttings in spring and early summer. Choose non-flowering, tender new shoots and remove a 10cm/4in length just above a bud on the parent plant.
CARE Leave the cuttings in water until roots appear, then transfer the cuttings to individual 9cm/3¹/₂in pots, filled with potting compost. Once plants reach about 15cm/6in in height, cut back the growing tips to help encourage bushy side growths.
HARVEST Pick young leaves when needed.

GOOSEBERRY CALENDAR

BUY Gooseberries begin to fruit in their second year, so it is best to buy two- to three-year-old bushes. Select a gooseberry bush with a clear stem of 10–15cm/4–6in and three to five main branches.
PLANT The best time to plant bare-root gooseberry bushes is late autumn so that they have time to establish before it gets too cold. Alternatively spring is fine, although planting in late spring will mean that the bushes make a slower start to the growing season. Pot-grown gooseberry bushes can be planted at any time of year, providing you avoid extreme conditions of very dry, wet or cold.
HARVEST Pick ripe fruits carefully because the skins burst easily.

BAKED GOOSEBERRIES
WITH LEMON VERBENA ICE CREAM & FLAPJACK

SERVES 6

INGREDIENTS

LEMON VERBENA ICE CREAM
Makes about 1.25 litres/2 pints
Vanilla pod
500ml/17¹/₂fl oz milk
100g/3¹/₂oz granulated sugar
4 egg yolks
10 fresh lemon verbena leaves – finger length
500ml/17¹/₂fl oz double cream, chilled

FLAPJACK
375g/13oz unsalted butter
100g/3¹/₂oz light brown soft sugar
300ml/10fl oz golden syrup
500g/1lb 1oz jumbo oats

BAKED GOOSEBERRIES
75g/2¹/₂oz unsalted butter
100g/3¹/₂oz soft brown sugar
500ml/17¹/₂fl oz gooseberries
Lemon juice, to taste
Dry sherry or marsala, to taste

TO SERVE
Small fresh lemon verbena leaves, to decorate

When he rubs lemon verbena leaves, Stephen recalls Michel Guérard's garden, where he was served a white peach poached in sweet wine accompanied by lemon verbena ice cream. He feels the gooseberry season is too short but always worth waiting for.

METHOD

1 **For the lemon verbena ice cream**, split the vanilla pod in half lengthways and scrape out the seeds. Combine the milk, vanilla seeds and pod and half the sugar in a large saucepan and bring to just below boiling point. Remove the pan from the heat, cover and leave for at least 15 minutes to allow the vanilla flavour to develop.

2 Meanwhile, in a large heatproof bowl, beat the egg yolks into the remaining sugar until the mixture is thick and pale. Bring the milk back to boiling point, then pour it on to the egg yolks and sugar, whisking steadily. Place the bowl over a saucepan of simmering water and, using a wooden spoon, stir the custard until it thickens; this takes 5–30 minutes. Remove the pan from the heat, add the lemon verbena leaves and plunge the base in a few centimetres of cold water. Leave to cool, stirring occasionally, until the mixture feels as if it has never been heated. Transfer the custard to a jug, leaving the vanilla bean in. Cover and chill.

3 When ready, strain the custard. Pour the custard and chilled cream into the ice cream machine and churn until it is the consistency of softly whipped cream. Scrape into freezer boxes, level and cover with greaseproof paper and a lid. Freeze overnight. Allow 15–20 minutes in the refrigerator before serving.

4 **For the flapjack**, preheat the oven to 180°C/350°F/gas mark 4. Line a baking sheet of 25 x 38cm (10 x 15in) with greaseproof paper. In a heavy-based saucepan, add the butter, sugar and syrup and bring to the boil. Add the oats and mix thoroughly. Pour into the tray and spread the mixture evenly. Bake in the oven for 20–25 minutes or until golden. Remove from the oven and allow to cool before tipping out, peeling off the paper and cutting into the desired size.

5 **For the baked gooseberries**, heat the butter in a nonstick saucepan. When it is bubbling add the sugar and gooseberries, turn up the heat and cook for 2 minutes until the butter and sugar have turned golden. Turn the heat down, add the lemon juice and sherry and cook for a further 2 minutes. Remove from the heat and keep warm.

6 **To serve**, spoon the gooseberries into a small dish. Dollop ice cream in a glass and decorate with freshly picked, small lemon verbena leaves. Serve the flapjack, cut into fingers, on the side.

4

PADSTOW KITCHEN GARDEN

Cornwall

After working in different careers, Jack Stein and Ross Geach have each returned to their family businesses: Jack to his father's, Rick Stein's, company, where he runs the development kitchen, and Ross to Trerethern Farm, just up the road from Padstow Harbour. Ross is the sixth generation of Geaches to work on their land. Although the lure of each of their 'firms' is easy to understand, it was their passion for seasonal Cornish produce that was integral to their decisions to come back to the family fold.

Jack is Ross's friend as well as colleague — they grew up together in Padstow, and Ross worked for ten years as a chef for Rick Stein. As a chef too, Jack appreciates the benefits of using fresh, locally sourced meat, fish and vegetables, not only for flavour and sustainability but also as an inspiration to create innovative recipes, where these ingredients shine. He is therefore keen to devise dishes that meet the challenges that Ross faces as a gardener: the bumper harvests followed by lean months; unexpected pests and diseases; and fluctuating manpower — all of which affect yields.

Where possible Jack's recipes use an ever-changing selection of herbs and crops that reflect the season and taste. This is a sensible approach to seasonality, given the scale of all of Rick Stein's enterprises: Rick Stein's Café feeds 150 at lunch; The Seafood Restaurant provides for 200 in the evening; and then there is the pub — The Cornish Arms — as well as Stein's Fish & Chips, Rick Stein's Fish in Falmouth and St Petroc's Bistro. It is a tall order for Ross to provide consistent quantities of any one crop.

OPPOSITE Ross and Jack are committed to showcasing the finest Cornish produce.
BELOW Geese wander around freely at Ross's family farm in Padstow, where he is the sixth generation to work the land.

The grower,
Ross Geach

The development chef,
Jack Stein

QUALITY CONTROL

There is also a procedure to follow with each new dish to the menu: Rick himself tastes and approves every new recipe, and any variations of it, before it can be introduced. However Rick's busy schedule often means he is unavailable, making it harder to respond quickly to a small harvest of one type of vegetable.

Ross finds there are advantages about having experience as a chef. He knows the type of vegetable and varieties chefs like to use — seasonality, taste, appearance and length of preparation time are all factors a chef might consider when choosing ingredients. He understands how to present his produce to a chef and, more fundamentally, knows exactly the best time to call or to deliver. This all sets Ross apart from other growers in a competitive market.

Ross's business, Padstow Kitchen Garden, has three main growing areas on the farm: three polytunnels; a field with spectacular views down the estuary; and his granddad's walled garden at the bottom of

the field. This final plot is where Ross reconnected with growing fruit and vegetables. He began helping his grandfather restore the walled garden in 2006. Old apple trees and blackcurrants were all that were left, apart from a mass of choking weeds. Clearing a patch of ground and sowing some rows of salad that thrived in the loamy Cornish soil gave Ross the gardening bug. That year he sold the salads but did not make a profit. The following year he and his grandfather cultivated the entire walled garden and with the proceeds Ross bought his first polytunnel. In 2008 they cleared the apple trees and blackcurrants to create more space for higher value, baby-leaf salads including: mizuna 'Red Knight'; mustards 'Red Giant', 'Red Lion', 'Red Frills', 'Pizzo', 'Red Zest' and 'Red Dragon'; pak choi 'Canton' and 'Rubi'.

With the proceeds Ross bought his second polytunnel and extended the crops to tomatoes, turnips, cucumbers, French beans, carrots, potatoes and beetroot. As his farm comprises more than 400 hectares/1,000 acres, there is huge potential for supplying his friend Jack within Rick Stein's enterprises.

BELOW Ross uses horticultural mesh, which lets rain and sun in, to protect his crops from pests and diseases.

ROSS & JACK'S
KITCHEN GARDEN SECRETS

- **Crop protection**: Cover outdoor crops with horticultural mesh. It is expensive but worth the initial outlay as it helps to create a microclimate (either by warming up the soil early or bringing on crops). It also lets in rain and sun while protecting plants from pests.
- **Pest control**: Scatter onion peelings in-between rows of turnips to keep moths away.
- **Ask for advice**: Ross talks to experts and uses the internet to research growing specific varieties.
- **Experiment**: Try different types of crops and their varieties. Grow crops that do well in your plot and do not persist with unsuccessful ones. The reasons for their failure are likely to be soil type, conditions or aspect, rather than your aptitude for growing.
- **Timing is all**: During hot summers make sure you do all the work and harvesting in the polytunnels early in the morning or in the evening when temperatures drop.

INDOOR TOMATOES

Among Ross's newer crops are tomatoes, of which he grows cordon, or vine, varieties supported on string as opposed to canes. He ensures the string is securely tied to a hook or crossbar in the polytunnel, but allows a little slack so that the plants can easily be twisted around the string, without any risk of the tension snapping the stem.

Ross always removes side shoots as they appear since they divert energy. He also pinches out each main stem's growing tip when seven trusses have set fruit; this is to encourage the plant to ripen the fruit rather than produce yet more trusses. Once the fruits appear Ross removes the leaves, three at a time starting from the base of each plant, to reveal the fruits and allow them to ripen in the full light.

FEED FOR FLAVOUR

The tomatoes are currently watered by hand, using a watering can, but this is very labour-intensive and can increase the risk of blossom end rot or the fruit splitting from lack of water, so Ross is hoping to install an irrigation system.

A home-made and diluted seaweed and comfrey feed is applied once a week, as opposed to the usual recommendation of every two weeks. He favours the 'little and often' approach to improve the flavour of the fruits and the health of the plants; irregular feeding can affect soil fertility, which in turn causes the fruits to split or be more susceptible to fungal

infection. Tomato blight can be a problem with indoor tomatoes, ruining a crop overnight. If the summer looks likely to be wet, Ross suggests using a preventative spray such as Bordeaux mix. Tomato leaf mould is another threat to indoor tomatoes, causing unsightly yellow blotches on fruit and a grey-brown mould on the leaves. Good ventilation will help – as will choosing a resistant tomato variety.

TRADITIONAL TURNIPS

Ross takes advantage of the excellent loamy Cornish soil at Trerethern Farm by growing turnips in the fields for the roots. He also uses containers to grow them for their tops, as turnips can be sown closely together and do not need to be thinned. Traditionally grown for a early and mid-spring harvest, they can be treated like cut-and-come-again crops and sown successively throughout the summer in a polytunnel.

Cabbage root fly is a big problem and Ross uses horticultural mesh to protect the seedlings from feeding larvae. The mesh also prevents flea beetle infestation, which leaves little holes in the tops of the turnips. Healthy strong plants are more likely to withstand attack from pests or diseases, so Ross encourages such growth by adding plenty of organic matter to the soil in autumn. Powdery mildew can be another problem for the turnip roots, but not the turnip tops, which are harvested when the leaves are young and fresh, before the fungal disease occurs. Heat and dry soil can cause the problems too, so Ross waters regularly and chooses a cool spot for his crop. A plant-and-fish oil or sulphur-based control is advisable if a white powdery deposit appears on turnip leaves.

TURBOT CHEEKS, PICKLED BEETROOT LEAVES & TURNIPS

SERVES 2

The inspiration for this dish came from the farm's waste products such as beetroot stems and turnip tops, which were previously composted. Turnips are a very traditional Cornish ingredient, appearing in many recipes from pasties to pies. Unfortunately, when they finally came through in late summer, the small turnips Ross was growing were not appreciated by the restaurants. They required too much preparation to be used as a side dish, so Jack came up with a dish that featured them as a main ingredient. Such a solution also helped reduce wastage in the kitchen – an important factor in a fine dining kitchen, where waste can be quite high. The brown butter dashi uses burnt butter solids from the bottom of the clarified butter pan, and the chorizo oil is the rendered fat from chorizo that Jack uses in his home-made sausage. Turbot cheeks are a delicious and underused part of this magnificent fish.

METHOD

1 Clean any sinew off the turbot cheeks, pat dry and season with the salt. Set aside.

2 **For the brown butter sauce**, melt the butter in a saucepan over a gentle heat. When bubbling, add the skimmed milk powder, cook until it starts to brown, then add the stock, dashi and kombu. Blitz the butter mix in a food processor and then pass through a sieve. Set aside to cool and then refrigerate. When the brown butter is cold a skin should form; remove this with a spoon, leaving the liquid behind. Put the liquid in a saucepan and reheat and then emulsify with the xanthan gum, using a stick blender. The consistency should be fairly thick. At this point, check the seasoning and adjust with salt if needed.

3 **For the pickled beetroot leaves and turnips**, quarter the turnips and cut the beetroot leaves into 5cm/2in pieces. Combine the remaining ingredients in a saucepan and warm through. Remove from the stove and add the turnip quarters and beetroot stems. Cool and then refrigerate for 2 hours.

4 **To serve**, cook the cheeks skin-side down in a nonstick frying pan. When you see the edges colour, add a knob of butter. Cook for about 1 minute, then flip them over and cook briefly on the other side. Remove from the pan and leave to rest. Cut small pieces of pickled beetroot stems and arrange under a slice of pickled turnip. Sauce each plate with the brown butter sauce and add the turbot cheeks, drizzle with chorizo oil and garnish with the turnip tops.

INGREDIENTS

240g/9oz turbot cheeks
Pinch of Cornish salt

BROWN BUTTER SAUCE
50g/2oz unsalted butter
1 tbsp skimmed milk powder
250ml/9fl oz fish stock
1 tsp dashi
10g/⅓oz kombu or dried seaweed
0.6g/¹/₅₀oz xanthan gum
Salt, to taste

PICKLED BEETROOT LEAVES
& TURNIPS
2 baby turnips
Beetroot leaves
200ml/⅓ pint cider vinegar
30g/1oz caster sugar
⅓ tsp sliced red chilli
½ tsp fennel seeds
Bay leaf
½ tsp sea salt
Rind of half a lime

TO SERVE
Knob of butter
Drizzle of chorizo oil (reserved when cooking chorizo)
6 small fresh turnip tops, to garnish

BRILL WITH HERITAGE TOMATO & WHITE MISO

SERVES 2

Things are not always perfect in the Padstow Kitchen Garden and at Trerethern Farm. Sometimes crops work and sometimes they do not, but both of these recipes try to allow for this and provide a place where crops can be used when and where they are ready. The combination of white miso and the Iberico ham trimmings taken from the black pig leg served at The Seafood Restaurant gives this dish a magnificently savoury flavour. The vegetables are barely cooked and then assembled at the last minute. Jack fermented his own miso using mushy peas and added a bit of this and off-the-shelf white miso to the chicken stock. His white miso is now a year old and tastes like a very Marmitey sake – it is quite odd but tasty. When the season moves on from using samphire as a garnish for this dish, it is replaced with nasturtium leaves and flowers. The lemon confit is a great way of getting acidity into the dish. Brill is not particularly strong in flavour, but its firm texture provides a great base for the small dice of vegetables. The tomatoes are different varieties, a little green, and are cut into concassé. They are added at the very end to give a burst of freshness to cut through the sauce.

INGREDIENTS

WHITE MISO CHICKEN STOCK
1 litre/1³/4 pints chicken stock
25g/1oz white miso

CONFIT LEMON
1 tbsp lemon rind
7 tsp lemon juice
1 tsp granulated sugar

TO SERVE
10g/¹/3oz peas
15g/¹/2oz courgette
15g/¹/2oz tomatoes, roughly chopped
80g/2¹/2oz brill pieces
Grapeseed oil
10g/¹/3oz butter, plus a a knob of
     butter to cook the ham
7g/¹/4oz Iberico ham
50ml/2fl oz white miso chicken stock
0.7g/¹/40oz confit lemon, finely diced
Samphire or nasturtium leaves and
     flowers, to garnish

METHOD

1   **For the white miso chicken stock**, warm the chicken stock and then add the white miso and blend.

2   **For the confit lemon**, place all of the ingredients in a small saucepan and cook at about 75°C/167°F for 30 minutes.

3   **To serve**, blanch the peas and courgettes for 30 seconds each and put aside, with the tomato concassé.

4   Meanwhile, sauté the brill in grapeseed oil, and finish with a little of the butter, at 45°C/113°F.

5   In another saucepan, add the ham with the knob of butter and cook for 2 minutes. Add the white miso chicken stock and the vegetables and reheat, then reduce by 10 per cent. To finish, emulsify the last of the butter and add the confit lemon.

6.   Lay half the vegetables and some white miso chicken stock on each plate, place the brill on top and garnish with the samphire or nasturtium leaves and flowers.

5

L'ENCLUME

Cumbria

L'Enclume is owned by Simon Rogan, a busy two-Michelin star chef who takes growing his own produce incredibly seriously. Simon's research and development centre, Aulis, experiments with produce, and this high-tech approach to developing food is both exciting and unfamiliar. His farm, called 'Our Farm', is both a working plot and a veg-grower's heaven – an array of polytunnels, raised beds and crates of seedlings. The uniformity and quality of produce are truly inspiring. Amid it all is the talented chef and grower Dan Cox. Dan taught himself to cultivate crops here, which is no mean feat given the difficulties with the soil and exposed position of the farm – not to mention the exacting standards demanded by Simon in the kitchen. Dan won the twenty-fifth Roux Scholarship, and when he is not knee-deep in mud at the farm he is Simon's right-hand-man and the chef/director of Aulis.

While some chefs are happy with a mere kitchen garden, Simon Rogan has his own farm to provide fresh seasonal ingredients for his restaurant empire. This 2.5-hectare/6-acre plot in the Cartmel Valley in Cumbria is testament to his desire to grow organic produce to near-perfect quality. If your cooking has been awarded two Michelin stars, you would inevitably demand the very best produce. (Indeed it was the varying quality of produce from his suppliers that spurred Simon to grow his own.) However, for Simon, growing is part of a wider ethos concerning produce, ensuring it is local, seasonal and organic. Influenced by chef Mark Veyrat, who bases his food around the flora of the Haute-Savoie region in France, Simon aims to use Cumbria as his larder.

AN INSPIRING APPROACH

When it comes to growing Simon talks about precision, which is not a term often used to describe sowing, growing and harvesting. But it is this approach, along with Simon's talent and creative flair, which enables the kitchen at L'Enclume, just 3 kilometres/2 miles from Our Farm, to support fifty covers a night of the most exciting, exquisite food.

Simon is a visionary too – he was using seasonal local food long before many could see its value. For him it is key that his team shares the same goals, dynamism and passion.

As well as being an accomplished chef, Dan has proved extraordinarily green-fingered. While a head chef in London he began by growing the 'unbuyables' in his own small garden and conservatory: borage flowers, anise hyssop and nasturtiums. In 2011 Dan was brought in to run Aulis and, despite being self-taught, oversaw the relationship between the kitchen and a local organic farm that provided produce for them. Expansion led to a change of plan, and Dan

Chef/director of Aulis and grower, **Dan Cox**

The chef, **Simon Rogan**

OPPOSITE A two-tiered barrier system was constructed to provide Our Farm with much-needed protection in its exposed position.

found himself at the helm of the project to set up Our Farm.

His uniform rows of lush crops, all thriving in raised beds, are astonishing and inspiring in equal measure. It only goes to show that if you have enthusiasm, commitment and a desire to produce great vegetables . . . everything is possible.

The stunning site is surrounded by the rolling Cumbrian hills of the Lake District and comes with issues that would overwhelm most growers: poor clay soil, waterlogging, and exposure to harsh easterly winds. Dan's approach was pragmatic: identify the problem and find a solution – most often from reading or researching on the internet.

He chose raised beds as the best way to work with the farm soil, and he filled these with a mixture of topsoil and green waste from the local area. He initially built the raised beds in a polytunnel, on a layer of membrane, but quickly regretted the decision as it created a barrier between the growing

medium and the earth, thereby closing off the benefit of microbiotic activity. The following winter he lifted all the raised beds, removed the membrane and rebuilt them directly on the earth.

Among Dan's first crops was a L'Enclume staple – good King Henry (*Chenopodium bonus-henricus*) – which is a key element of a signature duck dish; lovage (*Levisticum officinale*) too is always on the menu. Using the traditional method for an emulsion, Simon blanches lovage leaves and blitzes it to make a lovage oil and then feeds in a soft-boiled egg, blending it all together. He pairs this mixture with potatoes, onions and onion ashes (a combination of browned onions, rapeseed oil and maltodextrin).

Following the philosophy of 'if we have grown it, we use it all', the kitchen cooks the lovage stem too: chefs pull apart and blanch the stems before deep frying them to make lovage twigs.

Oyster plant (*Mertensia maritima*) is a recent success for Dan. An indigenous sea vegetable from the west coast of Scotland, the kitchen previously sourced it from a Dutch company as it could not be found in the UK. After dogged research, Dan tracked down a UK source for the plants.

BELOW LEFT Space is maximized in the polytunnels by growing seedlings on shelves suspended from the ceiling.
BELOW RIGHT An organized approach is fundamental to growing the finest-quality produce on Our Farm.

Today the restaurant creates dishes without using citrus (or bananas for that matter). But acidity is an essential ingredient to balance or lift dishes, so this is a considerable hole in the taste cupboard. This is where Aulis, the research centre, comes into its own. They discovered that pickles and vinegars bring the same acidity to a dish without having to rely on a lemon or lime.

STARTING FROM SCRATCH

Dan raises most of his crops from seed, and his propagation tunnel is like the heartbeat of the farm. It is beautiful, with row upon row of emerging seedlings. Uniformity rules in here too, with a rotation of seedlings that can be cropped as micro-leaves, including green orach and red Russian kale. Interestingly Simon and Dan prefer to grow on the shoots a little more than normal. It gives the roots and stems a more developed flavour, which they much prefer.

Simon and Dan encourage L'Enclume's chefs to help at the farm and to see what is in season. However it is Australian chef Lucia Corbel who is responsible for most of the harvesting and who runs the farm when Dan is off site. The combination of chef and grower works well: Lucia understands how the crops will be used — vital for timing harvests — and suggests ways to encourage younger chefs in Simon's team of twelve to respect the growing process and the produce.

Sustainability is a mantra for Simon and Dan and for their vision for Our Farm. A local spring provides the water, and a wind turbine produces the electricity for the polytunnels. Ever keen to progress, they are moving towards a biodynamic system of growing. This is not just because Simon sees this as an opportunity to have more control over sowing and harvesting crops — given that this is governed by the cycles of the moon when you grow biodynamically — but because of the potential benefits of crop health, yield and, of course, taste. Cows and pigs are the next on the list to receive the inimitable Our Farm treatment.

INDOOR CUCUMBERS

Crop health is a central concern for all produce grown by Dan, and this can be a particular problem with cucumbers. Indoor varieties can be trickier to grow, being more susceptible to pests and diseases, but as the fruits are longer and smoother than outdoor cucumbers Dan and Simon find ways to meet this challenge. They opt for F1 varieties if possible, as these do not produce male flowers (which otherwise need constant removing to ensure the female flowers are not pollinated, which results in bitter-tasting fruits). They choose high-yielding and tasty 'Iznik'; 'Dragon's Egg', which looks as it sounds and tastes like honeydew melon; and reliable 'Marketmore', which is resistant to powdery and downy mildew. Cucamelons are good too, and Dan and Simon also grow the gherkin cucumber varieties – perfect for pickling.

According to Dan, the trick with indoor cucumbers is to use strings to support the plants, rather than canes. As string or twine is more flexible it is less likely to damage the stems when twisting or tying them in. Pinch tips out when they reach the roof of the polytunnel or greenhouse. Also remove the tips of the side shoots two leaves beyond the female flowers (look for tiny fruits behind the blooms) and cut out the tips of flowerless side shoots when they are 60cm/24in long. If you do not have raised beds you can use growbags.

If powdery mildew becomes a problem, Dan sprays plants every week or two with a mix of one tablespoon baking soda with a teaspoon dormant oil and one teaspoon insecticidal or liquid soap (not detergent) in 4.5 litres/1 gallon water.

CUCUMBER CALENDAR

SOW Sow seeds of indoor cucumber varieties in a heated greenhouse from late winter to early spring, or in mid-spring in an unheated greenhouse.
PLANT Pot seedlings individually into 10cm/4in pots from early to late spring. When sturdy, transplant into their final positions.
HARVEST Do this from midsummer to mid-autumn, for baby or mature cucumbers.

FLAKY CRAB & CUCUMBER, MALLOW & YOUNG SQUID

SERVES 4

This very light, fresh dish marries together all that is great about produce in the L'Enclume vicinity. Superbly flaky Muncaster crab and young local squid is paired with the abundance of wild mallow foraged from the coast and the best cucumbers – flowers and shoots – picked daily from Our Farm.

METHOD

1   Boil the crab in salted water for 7 minutes. Chill in a blast chiller or ice water. When chilled, crack the crab and separate the brown and white meat from the shell. Season the white meat with some of the brown, then add salt to taste. Clean each squid by removing its head followed by the pen (the feather-shaped internal structure that supports the squid's mantle) and guts. Rinse then remove the fine skin and sinew. Dry and freeze; then cut into 1cm/½in squares and thaw. Peel, deseed and cut the cucumber into 1cm/½in cubes. If you have a vacuum packer, vacuum the cucumber to compress before you dice it.

2   **For the mallow soup**, sweat the onion until soft; add the cucumber and mallow leaves. Cook for 2 minutes. Add boiling stock, cream and ascorbic acid. Blend until smooth, pass through a sieve, season and chill over ice.

3   **For the squid croutons**, preheat the oven at 180°C/350°F/gas mark 4. Mix the yeast with the water and ferment at 42°C/107°F for 15 minutes. Mix the remaining ingredients with the fermented yeast and knead for 15 minutes. Prove in a warm place until the dough trebles in size. Knead for a further 2 minutes, divide into four and shape into four loaf tins. Cover and prove in a warm place until each dough piece trebles again. Bake for 25–30 minutes. When cool, break into little rough croutons and fry in a little clarified butter with salt until crispy.

4   **To serve**, mound some crabmeat in the centre of a plate. Spoon some seasoned raw squid on top and then place over some cucumber cubes. Spoon around some of the mallow soup, arranging the squid croutons, baby cucumbers, chrysanthemum shoots and mallow flowers on top. Finish with a drizzle of rapeseed oil and a sprinkle of sea salt.

INGREDIENTS

1 live medium crab
Salt
4 baby squids
¼ cucumber

MALLOW SOUP
150g/5oz onion, sliced
100g/3½oz cucumber, sliced
350g/12oz mallow leaves
750ml/1⅓ pints boiling vegetable stock
140ml/5fl oz whipping cream
1 tsp ascorbic acid
Salt and pepper

SQUID CROUTONS
50g/2oz dried yeast
250ml/9fl oz water
500g/1lb 1oz T55 bread flour
1 tbsp salt
100ml/3½fl oz olive oil
100ml/3½fl oz white wine vinegar
250ml/9fl oz squid ink
30g/1oz clarified butter

TO GARNISH
Baby cucumbers with their flowers
Chrysanthemum shoots
Mallow flowers
Rapeseed oil
Sea salt

DAN & SIMON'S
KITCHEN GARDEN SECRETS

- **Be resourceful**: Using materials he found on the farm Dan made his own cloches to cover the raised beds. They help to protect crops from rain.
- **Research well**: Dan spent about 60 hours sourcing oyster plants, and it was well worth the time.
- **Waste not**: If you have run out of room for your seedlings, think about other ways to use them. Dan plants spare red pak choi seedlings in growbags and leaves them to bolt so he can use the flowers.
- **Taste regularly**: Try crops at different stages to identify new flavours, and optimum times to pick. Dan discovered that turnip tops, for example, grew quickly after a heavy rainfall, resulting in a thick stem, but these stems were packed with flavour.
- **Harvesting**: Place your gathered veg in a bucket of cold water. This helps with the cleaning process and preserves quality, especially on hot days.
- **Protective heat**: Use a heat mat to propagate young shoots and young plants in modular trays. Using very gentle heat improves germination rates.

PEST-FREE CARROTS

Preventing attacks by carrot fly can be the key to growing healthy carrots. Ingeniously, Dan grows his carrots in raised beds, more than 60cm/24in from the ground. At this height the crop is well protected from ravages by carrot flies, which cannot fly that high. The bed's generous depth also helps to widen the range of carrots grown as, typically, rounder shorter varieties are recommended for shallower raised beds and containers. Dan is also a fan of propagation film but with one proviso: if it is left on the beds on a hot day, it will affect germination.

Carrots like a sunny spot and light, well-drained soil as they can split and fork if the soil is heavy clay. It therefore pays to start preparing the bed in winter, by digging in organic matter, because carrots do not like fresh manure. Remove any stones as you are digging in the manure.

Dan and Simon grow 'Sugarsnax', 'Paris Market Atlas', 'Yellowstone', 'Atomic Red', 'Purple Haze' and 'Sweet Candle' carrots. As the seeds are small, mix them with some sand so you can spot where they have been sown. This will aid drainage too and allow for thinner sowings. Ensure the soil is kept moist as too little water may result in woody roots. Harvest carrots in the evening to avoid attracting carrot fly.

Maincrop varieties can be stored, so lift them by mid-autumn and store in a box or container, in layers of sand. Keep an eye on them and remove any carrots that show signs of mould.

CARROT CALENDAR

SOW Sow early varieties in late winter and early spring under cloches. Sow maincrop varieties from mid-spring to midsummer. Sow seed 10cm/4in deep, 15cm/6in apart. It is worth sowing thinly to avoid the need for thinning (which attracts carrot fly unless the bed is higher than 60cm/24in).
HARVEST Do this from late spring onwards. When roots are tiny they are packed with flavour.

'PARIS MARKET' & 'SUGARSNAX' CARROTS WITH HAM FAT CREAM & NASTURTIUM

SERVES 4

This dish is seen as a L'Enclume classic, and its conception was triggered by the harvesting of their first-ever carrots. The ham fat cream gives a strong umami richness, bringing out the true sweetness of the carrots and unifying the mouthfeel of all the different carrot textures.

METHOD

1   Blanch the carrots in salted boiling water for 1 minute, refresh in ice water and lightly scrape off the skins.

2   **For the carrot purée**, peel and slice the carrots into 1cm/½in pieces, then combine with the carrot juice. Boil until the carrots are soft and all the juice has evaporated. Season with salt, and blend until smooth.

3   **For the carrot crisp**, mix all the ingredients together, spread paper-thin on to a silicone mat and bake at 110°C/225°F/gas mark ¼ for 12 hours. Leave the carrot crisp to cool.

4   **For the ham fat cream**, bring the ham stock to a simmer, then blitz with the diced ham fat, until smooth, in a blender. Pass through a fine sieve, return to the blender, add the xanthan gum and blitz again. Pass again and allow to cool.

5   **For the tarragon oil**, blend the oil and tarragon at 65°C/150°F for 6 minutes. Sieve and chill over ice.

6   **To serve**, place a generous smear of ham fat cream on each plate with three or four nice blobs of carrot purée. Dress the 'Sugarsnax' carrots and 'Paris Market' carrots in a little rapeseed oil, season and arrange four carrots of each variety on the plate. Add shards of carrot crisp, the herbs and flowers, and finish with a drizzle of tarragon oil and sea salt.

INGREDIENTS

16 'Sugarsnax' carrots
16 'Paris Market' carrots
Salt

CARROT PURÉE
500g/1lb 1oz carrots
750ml/1⅓ pints carrot juice
Salt

CARROT CRISP
100g/3½oz carrot purée
1 tbsp icing sugar
1 tbsp maltodextrine

HAM FAT CREAM
250ml/9fl oz ham stock
200g/7oz cured ham fat, diced
⅓ tsp xanthan gum

TARRAGON OIL
200ml/⅓ pint rapeseed oil
300g/10oz fresh tarragon

TO GARNISH
Rapeseed oil
Purslane
Nasturtium leaves
Nasturtium flower
Baby 'Fuji' spinach leaves
Sea salt

6

THE FELIN FACH GRIFFIN

Powys

Growing seasonal produce for the exciting, innovative and award-winning kitchen at The Griffin is as much about providing excellent flavour and variety as ensuring that every square metre of earth yields as much as possible. For head gardener Joe Hands, having a kitchen garden is not a public-relations or cost-saving exercise; when seeds, equipment, labour, upkeep and crop failure are taken into account, they are actually more costly than buying in produce. For Joe and The Griffin's chef, Ross Bruce, however, what is important is seasonality of crops, what thrives in the heavy clay soil of the Brecon Beacons, interesting varieties and organic wholesome produce.

In 2009 Joe was charged with creating a garden to supply The Griffin with seasonal produce. To do this he had to transform a 0.4-hectare/1-acre field that had once been a dumping ground for bricks, rubble and rubbish. Joe took a step-at-a-time approach in clearing the ground and methodically worked over the area for two years, planting potatoes in each new bed and adding plenty of organic matter to open up the clay soil. Because he was aiming for organic certification from The Soil Association during this time, the work had to be done by hand and without using chemicals to remove troublesome weeds.

Within Joe's vegetable plot Ross was given his own small area when he first joined The Griffin in 2010 as sous chef. Nowadays, since becoming head chef, Ross considers it a 'luxury' to be in the productive garden, even if it is for a mid-service harvest of salad leaves. His genuine passion works so well with Joe's that he has real empathy if any of Joe's crops fail or are affected by bad weather or pests. However Ross has learned to adapt quickly and create a new menu around the crops that are doing well. Though they make the seed order together, their collaboration is generally more organic. If Ross wants to try something new, change a variety or harvest something early, he is able to discuss it with Joe, who is on hand every day.

FELIN FACH'S FAVOURITES

For Ross, peas are an essential ingredient, so among the crops thriving in the productive garden is the early summer pea 'Telephone' from Italy, which is both a good cropper – 80kg/187lb being a typical annual yield – and delicious to eat. This success has given Joe the opportunity to trial other pea varieties in the hope of staggering the harvest time. Another important crop is squash, which he finds versatile, tasty and great for storing.

When it comes to brassicas Joe and Ross choose heritage varieties (cavolo nero and Russian kale) for their taste and the benefits of having a reliable harvest. Joe finds it unsatisfactory to grow crops

The grower,
Joe Hands

The chef,
Ross Bruce

OPPOSITE As well as providing fresh eggs, the chickens at Felin Fach help keep slugs at bay in the vegetable plot.

such as asparagus, because they occupy considerable space for only a small yield and they also require a lot of weeding.

Characteristically Joe and Ross also experiment with possible new sources of ingredients. Ross for example suggested they try growing chervil root (*Chaerophyllum bulbosum*) – a delicious crop with a delicate flavour of white chocolate and parsnip. It hails from the mountains of eastern France and central Europe and is almost impossible to buy in the UK. Chervil root is tricky to grow as it needs sub-freezing temperatures to germinate, so Joe uses the freezer to create the appropriate conditions for its seeds to flourish. In Ross's opinion, Joe is slowly perfecting the crop, although the balance of starch and sugar in the roots is still not quite right, and this affects the texture and taste when blitzed to a purée.

Raspberries grow well along the shady boundary hedge of the plot, as do strawberries and currants.

ALL-YEAR GARLIC

One of Joe's favourite crops is garlic, because it is planted when the garden is quiet, it can be interplanted with spinach to maximize each bed's productivity and it is then lifted to make room for another crop such as onions or a late leek variety. Technically, from a crop rotation point of view, Joe admits he should not plant so intensively in one spot, but given garlic's relatively shallow root system his system does not appear to have caused residual problems with pests or disease.

Joe grows garlic 'Albigensian Wight', a soft-neck variety, which Ross likes for its mellow flavour and versatility. Nine beds each year are given over to garlic, with one bed untouched to harvest cloves to plant the following season. Having this many beds allows Ross to gather bulblets in early spring to use like spring onions. Though Ross includes some garlic flowers in dishes, very few garlic plants are left in the soil to reach full maturity. Instead they are taken to the kitchen when the bulbs are little more than clove sized. Larger-sized bulbs are perfect for roasting.

OPPOSITE The vegetable garden is quite literally a minute's walk from the kitchen at The Griffin.

GARLIC CALENDAR

PLANT Before planting garlic in late autumn or early winter, Joe adds well-rotted donkey manure to the plot. (This is typical of his practical gardening approach – there is a donkey sanctuary just up the road.) He then covers the beds in black plastic mulch matting, which helps to keep down weeds. He makes slits, about 30cm/12in apart, in the matting and through these holes he plants individual cloves just below the surface.
CARE Depending on weather conditions, rust can appear on the garlic plants, but once their leaves are removed the crop itself is not affected and can still be used in the kitchen.
HARVEST Pick whenever you need – from 'wet', or first-crop, garlic to end-of-season, large cloves.

ONIONS FROM SETS

In much in the same way as Joe prepares the beds for garlic, he digs plenty of well-rotted donkey manure into the onions beds. He grows from sets to save time, and he often overwinters them before planting them out in late winter. He has experimented with a mid-autumn planting to see if it improves yield or flavour, but has been met with varying degrees of success. Joe prefers 'Snowball' onions, even though this firm large white variety is prone to bolt – but it is hard to tell if that is due to variety or conditions.

ONION CALENDAR

SOW When Joe sows his onion sets in late winter he suspends the seed trays off the ground using a ladder-like shelf and hangs a tray in between each rung. It is a tried-and-tested way of preventing slugs and snails from decimating an onion crop.
PLANT In mid- and late spring he transplants the young plants into well-drained soil in a sunny spot, where they thrive. As with garlic cloves, he makes slits in black plastic mulch matting and plants through that to help suppress weeds and maintain soil moisture.
HARVEST Ross likes to use some of the onions when quite small. Joe lifts the rest of the crop when the foliage turns yellow, and he leaves them on the ground to allow the skins to harden. If it is wet, he brings the onions indoors and dries them in a cool airy place.

WET GARLIC BARIGOULE

SERVES 4

Barigoule is a traditional method of cooking globe artichokes that are to be served as a garnish and occasionally as a dish in itself. Ross's initial inspiration for his barigoule dish came from a mixture of frustration, starvation and the fact that globe artichokes are not grown at The Griffin. He then realized that a peeled globe artichoke has an almost identical shape and size to a bulb of wet, or immature, garlic. This is a head of easy-to-grow standard garlic that has been picked early so that it has not had time to form a more recognizable bulb. Wet garlic is scarcely for sale anywhere and seldom seen at markets, so if you do not grow it you might just miss out. In terms of flavour, wet garlic is gentler and much less bitter than fully mature garlic, allowing you to eat a whole head or more in a single sitting. This dish calls for up to 3 heads per person, and the garlic effect may linger for up to 4 hours.

Nearly all of the wet garlic barigoule recipe can be adapted according to personal taste and the availability of ingredients. Ross has included some items that have been stored over winter, and others that were fresh out of the ground.

INGREDIENTS

2 tblsp rapeseed oil
100g/3½oz butter
400g/12oz pancetta, skin removed and divided into 4
4 small red onions
4 small carrots – if very fresh just cut away the leaves
12 bulbs of plump and well-rounded wet garlic,
      cut to 10cm/4in long
4 sticks of celery, peeled and each cut into 2 or 3 pieces,
      or 4 small handfuls of lovage
2 tsp fresh thyme leaves
Salt and pepper
250ml/9fl oz white wine
Parmesan cheese rind, cut into 4

PICKLED SHALLOTS
4 large banana shallots
50g/2oz caster sugar
200ml/⅓ pint white wine vinegar
100ml//3½fl oz water
Pinch of salt

TO SERVE
Rapeseed oil
Handful of podded fresh peas
Handful of fresh mangetout
Large tomato, peeled and deseeded
Fresh thyme, to garnish
Handful of thinly sliced radishes, to garnish

METHOD

1 Heat a large, thick-based saucepan and add a little oil and a good knob of butter. When the butter begins to foam, add the pieces of pancetta and cook for a few minutes on a low heat. Mix in the onions, carrots, garlic, celery and thyme, season well with salt and cook for 5 minutes. Pour in a good slug of wine, cheese rind and enough hot water to cover everything by about 2.5cm/1in, check the seasoning and cover with a lid of greaseproof paper. Bring to the boil, then simmer very gently for 1 hour. Remove from the heat and allow everything to cool in the liquid.

2 **For the pickled shallots**, slice the shallots to make rings, keeping all the middles for something else. Heat the sugar, vinegar, water and salt in a saucepan. Once everything has dissolved, add the shallots and remove from the heat.

3 **To serve**, remove the pancetta and some of the garlic from the saucepan of barigoule. Split the garlic right through the middle lengthways; set aside. Bring the barigoule saucepan up to a simmer, making sure that everything is hot enough to serve. In a large frying pan, heat a little oil and start to caramelize the pancetta, then the garlic. At the very last minute, add the peas, mangetout and tomato to the barigoule saucepan. Divide the contents equally between 4 plates, making sure each one has a bit of everything. Garnish with thyme, pickled shallots and radish slices.

WILD ROCKET

One crop that is great for any productive garden is wild rocket (*Diplotaxis tenuifolia*), because it is a cut-and-come-again plant and so can be harvested season after season. Another bonus is that, being perennial, it does not have to be sown and tended each year. Wild rocket has a stronger flavour than the common variety and a deeper green leaf colour. Originally sown and grown in a modular tray by Joe, to help encourage good root systems, these plants are thereafter low-maintenance plants, requiring only to have woody growth cut back each year and surrounding soil kept weed-free.

From early to midsummer, flea beetle may be a pest – piercing wild rocket leaves. Joe recommends being vigilant for the very first signs and, if spotted, covering the plants with horticultural fleece. Joe has even been known to cover the crop at an earlier stage in the season, in an attempt to prevent attack by flea beetles. He also suggests holding sticky tape just above the rocket leaves and then stamping on the ground – the smaller-than-a-pinhead beetles are said to jump on to the sticky-tape 'trap'.

WILD ROCKET CALENDAR

SOW Thinly sow directly into the ground from mid-spring to midsummer in 1cm/½in drills.
CARE Thin seedlings to about 30cm/12in apart.
HARVEST Pick young leaves, choosing a few from each plant rather than cropping from just one plant at a time. Protect late summer sowings with a cloche to prolong the chances for harvest until winter.

JOE & ROSS'S
KITCHEN GARDEN SECRETS

- **Listen to the season**: If it is wet and cold, but you should technically be sowing, hold off from doing so until the weather has warmed a little. By doing this you help to ensure seeds germinate optimally and seedlings grow well.
- **Beat pests**: Joe has cleverly rigged up a ladder, suspended from the main frame of the polytunnel. The seed trays fit snugly between each rung of the ladder, ensuring slugs and snails do not get a chance to munch the seedlings.
- **Save space**: Be creative – think about varieties that can be interplanted, to boost your plot's productivity.
- **Collect rainwater**: Connect drainpipes to water butts from as many roofs as possible – a shed and greenhouse roof will work just as well as a house to collect water run-off.
- **Use guttering**: Sow seeds of crops like leeks and garlic in lengths of guttering. It saves time when it comes to planting out – just slide out the soil and seedlings into a prepared shallow trench.

SCORCHED ONION WITH CRISPY ROCKET & PESTO

SERVES 4 AS A SIDE DISH

This is a really easy recipe that is also very versatile and can be served alone or as part of something else. Ross loves to put it on the table with roast lamb or baked fish, but he also serves it as the main component of many vegetarian dishes. As the 'petals' of the onion become very delicate, Ross always serves scorched onion in the dish it was cooked in.

METHOD

1 **For the scorched onion**, preheat the oven to 240°C/475°F/gas mark 9. When peeling the onion from the root to the tip, be careful to keep the root intact and flat so that the bulb can stand upright without any help. With a sharp knife, cut through the top towards the base as if you were halving it, but leave 2cm/³/₄in uncut. Turn the onion, as if you were to cut it into quarters and cut again. Repeat the process until you have eight cuts, always making sure the bottom 2cm/³/₄in is intact. Dress the onion well with olive oil, trying to get some into the middle. Place on an attractive roasting tray that is large enough for the bulb to open like a flower. Bake for about 15 minutes. Then turn the oven down to 180°C/350°F/gas mark 4, and season the middle of the onion, which will have opened up, with salt and pepper. Bake for a further 20 minutes, basting with the juices every so often.

2 **For the pesto**, blitz all ingredients together either by hand in a pestle and mortar or in a food processor to your desired coarseness. Season with salt.

3 **For the crispy rocket**, prepare the ingredients to go into the oven when you turn the scorched onion down to 180°C/350°F/ gas mark 4. Toss the rocket with a drizzle of oil and season with salt. Lay out in a single layer on a baking sheet and bake for 5–10 minutes.

4 **To serve**, spoon the pesto over the scorched onion and scatter with the crispy rocket leaves.

INGREDIENTS

SCORCHED ONION
Biggest onion you can find
Olive oil
Salt and pepper

PESTO
100g/3¹/₂oz rindless fresh Parmesan cheese
4 garlic cloves, chopped
Handful of toasted pine nuts
Large handful of fresh rocket
Olive oil
Salt

CRISPY ROCKET
Large handful of fresh rocket
Olive oil
Salt

7

THE PIG HOTEL

Hampshire

It is arguable that chef James Golding's decision to source produce for The Pig Hotel within a 40-kilometre/25-mile radius kick-started the food provenance revolution, not just because it was an original concept but also because it was James's vision, passion and enthusiasm that forced people to stop and think. Suddenly the number of kilometres that a cow had been reared from the restaurant where it would make its final appearance was valuable information for the menu.

The trend for local sourcing started with meat and game, but it is exciting to see the ethos has now extended to the kitchen garden. Even the sign at The Pig's entrance promotes 'kitchen garden food'. The hotel's gardener, Ollie Hutson, is an enthusiastic, wild-at-heart genius – with a penchant for carnivorous 'pest control' plants and slow worms and for ensuring that his chillies behave as perennials rather than annuals.

The edible paradise at The Pig is a walled garden of 0.15-hectares/$^1/_3$ acre comprising a tomato tunnel, a greenhouse, a fruit cage and perennial beds. Just

a few steps from the hotel, it collectively provides up to 85 per cent of the fruit, vegetables and herbs used in the kitchen. In the world of restaurant home-grown produce, this is an impressive statistic, and it is the result of hard work, organization, creativity and commitment. At The Pig, the kitchen garden is as much a guest experience as a productive plot. It is also somewhere for the hotel team to get their hands dirty – volunteering in the garden is encouraged.

For James, the satisfaction never dulls in knowing that a raw product comes in from the garden and is transformed by his team and served to a customer a few hours later. Yet James and Ollie are aware that there is a balance to strike when it comes to growing and supplying a kitchen. If there is too much produce, you risk waste; if not enough, you have to rely too much on suppliers – an additional and, most

OPPOSITE Fresh food from the kitchen garden inspires James's contemporary British seasonal menu.
BELOW Home-grown produce is central to The Pig Hotel's philosophy, and guests are encouraged to visit the gardens.

The grower,
Ollie Hutson

The chef,
James Golding

likely, unbudgeted expense. They are both keen that Ollie is treated as a supplier, receiving feedback and requests for crops the kitchen would like to try.

Ollie grows eye-catching crops such as Egyptian walking onions, Bulgarian giant leeks and tree spinach alongside more typical carrots, broad beans, peas, potatoes and beetroot. Experimenting with varieties also gives him a bit of challenge as to the choice of variety or the way the crop is used. Simply by tasting, Joe and James discovered that cavolo nero is delicious when it has bolted, just before it flowers. Its flavour is actually sweet and nutty and well worth using in the kitchen, so this plant is no longer consigned to the compost at this point in its life cycle.

Joe has adopted a creative approach for the winter months too, transforming the greenhouse from a propagation to a salad leaf nursery. Ollie removes the pea shale, used for drainage on the benches during the summer, lays heating cable and covers them with soil, thereby making shallow beds. He then sows beetroot, chard, edible chrysanthemums, 'Bright Lights' chard and claytonia to be used as a much-welcomed garnish during the winter months.

His latest method is to sow tight rows to create mini- rather than micro-leaves.

A regular feature on the menu at The Pig is agretti (*Salsola soda*), which is also known as beard of the monk or saltwort. It is much like samphire, with a strong mineral flavour. James likes to use the crop in all its growing stages. Fortunately agretti thrives in the walled garden.

GLOBE ARTICHOKES

A popular vegetable on The Pig's early summer menu is globe artichoke, so it earns a place in the kitchen garden's perennial beds. Once established, the plants are easy to grow and will produce a steady supply of tasty flower buds, which are otherwise an expensive ingredient to buy from suppliers.

Ollie plants 'Vert de Laon' and 'Green Globe' in rows, to maximize the yield. He suggests removing the leading shoot in the plant's first year, to encourage a bushy habit, and he mulches around the plants with manure before winter. Every three years he lifts and divides the plants to revive and increase stocks (it is easy to do – Ollie uses a sharp bread knife). He will not harvest in the first year after splitting, so removes globes as soon as they appear to help the plants build up strength.

Though traditionally slugs are the main pest that will eat globe artichokes and you can get aphid damage, neither has been a problem at The Pig so far.

GLOBE ARTICHOKE CALENDAR

SOW Do this from early to mid-spring in 10cm/4in pots, or in a seedbed insert 2–3 seeds in a hole 10cm/4in deep, with 30cm/12in between holes. When the seedlings have about five leaves, transplant to at least 60cm/24in apart.
PROPAGATE From early to mid-spring propagate globe artichokes from a root sucker from an established plant, removing pieces 20–30cm/8–12in long with at least two shoots to each section.
HARVEST Harvest when the flowers are the size of golf balls, before they begin flowering, and watch out for the spikes – they are lethal!

SILKY SEAKALE

It is interesting how vegetables come in and out of fashion. Where once seakale (*Crambe maritima*) was known as poor man's asparagus, these days you can expect to pay around £50 for 1kg/2lb 3oz of it. For centuries, locals have forced abundantly growing supplies under makeshift piles of pebbles on the beach, but salt-tolerant seakale will also grow inland, away from the coast. It is often forced like rhubarb and grown in the dark, to produce sweet tender stems in spring.

Seakale is an herbaceous perennial and can be picked year after year. Ollie has sown both wild and shop-bought seakale seeds. Although the shop-bought ones suffered low germination rates, he is philosophical and understands this can and does happen with seeds. He makes the point that this sort of outcome can turn beginners off growing, who blame a lack of horticultural prowess rather than non-viable seeds.

To build up stocks of his seakale, Ollie also propagates by root (or thong) cuttings in early winter. He pots up pieces of root, each 5cm/2in long, in compost mixed with plenty of horticultural grit – seakale likes free-draining soil. A year later, in winter, he plants them out in beds, to force them, ready for an early spring harvest of tender stems.

James is a huge fan of the crop, but the difference between the salty, mineral-rich wild seakale and their own produce, which is much more delicate in flavour, has resulted in Ollie experimenting with watering his crops with seawater to increase flavour. He has also mulched them with seaweed (both 'quickly' composted and fresh off the beach) – but in truth he has found little or no difference in taste to date.

SEAKALE CALENDAR

SOW From mid-spring to early summer, sow seeds 2.5cm/1in deep into well-drained soil in a sunny spot.
CARE Dig a couple of generous spadefuls of grit into the soil prior to planting, and keep the plot well watered while your plants establish. Apart from this, seakale needs only hard pruning in late autumn, by cutting the plants down to ground level.
HARVEST Leave plants to establish for three growing seasons before forcing and harvesting them.

BELOW In winter, dig up the seakale (1); cut the root (or thong) into 5cm/2in pieces (2); pot into a free-draining compost, adding horticultural grit to help improve the soil structure; (3) and plant out a year later.

OLLIE & JAMES'S
KITCHEN GARDEN SECRETS

- **Make your own**: Because of the benefits of home-made compost on the soil, Ollie is an avid composter, both in terms of recycling and reusing. He uses a three-bay system, turning each pile every month.
- **Boost fertility**: Ollie feels that the soil is so intensively cultivated at The Pig that it is essential to keep feeding and replenishing nutrients. He therefore digs in well-rotted manure as deep as possible, to help hold water and improve the soil's condition.
- **Try biological controls**: If you are growing in a greenhouse, conservatory or polytunnel why not adopt biological methods to control pests and diseases? Ollie experiments with carnivorous plants too and recommends *The Savage Garden: Cultivating Carnivorous Plants* by Peter d'Amato as a carnivorous-plant grower's bible.
- **Grow reserve crops**: Keep a back-up supply of crops. In recent years, with such wet springs and summers, mildew and slugs have been a problem with the legumes. Extra seedlings proved to be essential in the battle to maintain a supply of healthy plants.
- **Good neighbours**: Plant crops such as blueberries and cranberries together as they like the same (ericaceous) soil and conditions. Cranberries are creepers and blueberries grow on upright woody stems, so position them alternately. Together they maximize use of space and provide twice the yield in one area.

SEAKALE WITH BROWN SHRIMPS
& LEMON BUTTER SAUCE

SERVES 2

INGREDIENTS

Bunch of forced English seakale
Salt
Handful of fresh lava weed
Pot marigold petals. to garnish
LEMON BUTTER SAUCE
150g/5oz unsalted English butter
Half a lemon
Shallot, chopped
Generous handful of flat leaf parsley, chopped
100g/3½oz peeled brown shrimps
Salt and pepper

James loves this dish as it represents the beginning of summer for him. He and Ollie force the seakale at The Pig so they are able to let guests taste this 'poor man's asparagus' without worrying about depleting the wild coastal stocks. The shrimps and lemon butter sauce make perfect accompaniments, and the crispy lava weed adds a tasty texture to the dish.

METHOD

1   Blanch the seakale in salted boiling water until tender and place on a plate. Ensure the lava weed is thoroughly dry before deep-frying it until it turns light golden brown.

2   **For the lemon butter sauce**, place the butter in a saucepan and bring to the boil; watch the butter and when you see a golden brown covering starting to appear on the bottom of the saucepan add the lemon juice, then the shallot pieces, parsley, shrimps and seasoning.

3   **To serve**, pour the lemon butter sauce over the cooked kale and garnish with the petals of pot marigold.

MIXED GARDEN ARTICHOKE
& NANNY CHEDDAR SALAD

SERVES 2

INGREDIENTS

4 baby globe artichokes
Juice of 2 lemons
2 generous sprigs of rosemary
2 garlic cloves
250g/9oz Jerusalem artichokes
Rapeseed oil, for drizzling
Salt and pepper

DRESSING
500ml/17$\frac{1}{2}$fl oz sweet New Forest cider
2 tbsp Dijon mustard
1 tbsp cider vinegar
100ml/3$\frac{1}{2}$fl oz rapeseed oil

TO SERVE
Borage flowers, to garnish
50g/2oz goats' cheddar shavings, to
    garnish
Bunch of flowering mizuna, to garnish

This dish includes the best the garden at The Pig has to offer during summer and autumn. It combines semi-pickled globes, goats' cheddar and a sweet New Forest cider dressing in a salad that really does have those great sweet-and-sour notes, and is enhanced by a nice big ball of spicy mizuna.

METHOD

1   Preheat the oven to 180°C/350°F/gas mark 4. Cook the globe artichokes in a saucepan of boiling water seasoned with the lemon juice, a sprig of rosemary and a garlic clove. Cook until tender, then allow to cool. Halve the Jerusalem artichokes and put on a baking sheet, drizzle with rapeseed oil and sprinkle with the remaining rosemary sprig and remaining garlic clove, chopped. Season and roast for 20 minutes.

2   **For the dressing**, reduce the cider by three-quarters by boiling hard. Once the cider has cooled it should resemble golden syrup (if not add 1 tsp caster sugar and reboil until ready). Put the mustard, vinegar and 1 tsp reduced cider liquor into a food processor. Slowly add the oil until it comes together; if the dressing is too thick, slowly add some warm water.

3   **To serve**, dress the plate and layer all the ingredients together to look attractive. Garnish with fresh borage flowers, the cheese shavings and the flowering mizuna.

8

THE STAR INN

Yorkshire

Chef Andrew Pern regards Yorkshire as his larder, which provides all he needs to run his successful, fourteenth-century, thatched pub, The Star Inn, in the north Yorkshire village of Harome. It might be a bold claim, but you can see his point of view when you consider the rich variety of produce that is right on his doorstep: poultry, game and prize-winning beef; shellfish from the North Sea; apples from Nunnington Hall; seasonal produce from Helmsley Walled Garden; soft fruit from the Vale of York; and rhubarb from Wakefield.

Growing up on a farm in Whitby, just under an hour's drive across the North York Moors National Park from The Star Inn, Andrew has been surrounded by this exceptional food all his life. He helped his grandfather on his allotment and to run the 'rough' shoot on the family farm. He was also a keen fisherman on the River Esk. Unsurprisingly many of the best local suppliers are his childhood friends. Andrew honed his understanding and appreciation of good quality and seasonality by training under some of our very best chefs (he is a Roux scholar) and by working in France.

Since buying The Star Inn in 1996 Andrew has celebrated this close connection with the surrounding landscape and local producers by including the provenance of each ingredient on his menus: hand-picked village wild garlic or Pickering watercress or Harome honey-baked ham or garden-lovage hollandaise.

Jo Campbell, formerly kitchen gardener for Andrew Fairlie's two-Michelin star restaurant at Gleneagles, first met Andrew in 2003. At the time she was working at a nearby private estate in Thirsk, where she had renovated their splendid Victorian walled garden and transformed it into a productive plot. Such was her success that they were harvesting more fresh fruit and vegetables than the family could eat, so Jo began selling it in the local area. After arriving at the kitchen door of The Star Inn one day, offering a basket of beautifully presented and labelled rhubarb 'Timperley Early', Andrew agreed to take whatever Jo could supply.

NEW BEGINNINGS

In 2007 Andrew finally persuaded Jo to create a kitchen garden for The Star Inn in her spare time. She has since left Yorkshire, having spent three years as head vegetable gardener at Raymond Blanc's Le Manoir aux Quat'Saisons, and is now in Scotland. However Jo still helps Andrew choose the varieties for his veg plot at the start of each growing season and oversees the planting plans to supply the kitchen with 45 per cent of the produce required for a thousand covers a week.

The grower,
Jo Campbell

The chef,
Andrew Pern

OPPOSITE Jo and Andrew work closely together to plan the garden for the year ahead.

Jo is one of a small number of professional kitchen gardeners who approaches her work through the eyes of a chef, as opposed to a horticulturist. Choosing vegetables is more about the flavour and how it looks rather than its resistance to disease. For inspiration she looks through recipe books rather than growing guides.

She passionately believes a grower should spend time in the kitchen to see how vegetables and fruit are prepared and used. Likewise a chef should go into the kitchen garden to understand the growing process. She has met a surprising number of chefs who struggle to recognize the flower from Florence fennel or the tops of a leek or how sprouts grow.

For The Star Inn, Jo created a potager, with its classic combination of formal structure softened by loose planting. It is both productive, to satisfy the kitchen's demands, and pretty, for guests to enjoy wandering around. Jo especially enjoys sharing tips and offering advice to visitors. In this shared garden Andrew's only stipulation was that Jo made space

for a 3.5m/12ft table, made from a single piece of oak. This quirky, alternative-style 'chef's table' was be located in the heart of the kitchen garden, so guests really understood the link between garden and kitchen.

The site for the potager was previously a field so the soil was good for growing. Once the grass had been removed Jo just added locally sourced organic matter (they now make their own compost). The garden is also sheltered, which helps to buffer strong winds and harsh conditions. Though initially there was not enough space for a greenhouse or polytunnel, there are plans to accommodate one or the other. Initially Jo started crops off in her own greenhouse, but for more recent planting plans she has taken the current lack of a protected building into consideration and so has chosen varieties that can be direct sown.

Andrew is an avid seed catalogue reader, and Jo encouraged him to create his own wish list – something she recommends all chefs, and indeed any grower, should do before diving in and ordering a mountain of seeds. Featuring in the top section of Andrew's list were micro-herbs; these really benefit from being used within an hour or so of harvesting.

BELOW LEFT The Star Inn, a fourteenth-century longhouse, is situated on the edge of the North Yorkshire Moors.
BELOW RIGHT Andrew Pern commissioned willow sculptures for his vegetable garden.

In addition they are expensive to buy – and then their small tender leaves often lack flavour. Edible flowers, wild strawberries and courgette flowers were some of the other 'must-haves', again due to the flavour and quality that can be sourced and their high value.

To satisfy Andrew's needs, Jo created two edible-flower beds, filling them with pot marigolds (*Calendula officinalis*), rocket (*Eruca vesicaria* subsp. *sativa*), nasturtiums (*Tropaeolum majus*), cornflowers (*Centaurea cyanus*) and violets (*Viola odorata*) as well as introducing Andrew to white, rather than the traditional blue, borage (*Borago officinalis* 'Alba'), which took up another of the smaller beds. Andrew and Jo also agreed on planting squash, purple sprouts and a variety of kales, including cavolo nero.

In Jo's opinion, cavolo nero is a great example of how chefs and gardeners approach growing and harvesting in completely different ways – chefs preferring to take cavolo nero leaves when they are young, small and tender. They are interested in trying crops at all stages of growth and letting the flavour determine the time to harvest rather than when tradition dictates. From a gardener's point of view, cavolo nero is likely to be left in the ground over winter, by which time it will have matured and produced large leaves. Jo is excited by the chef's approach, because their experimentation introduces new textures and flavours into the kitchen and broadens the way a crop is used.

Preparation of a crop is another consideration that determines what a chef will want in the kitchen. Jerusalem artichokes, for example, can be knobbly and fiddly to prepare, or be smooth-skinned and easy-to-peel like 'Fuseau'.

Another advantage for chefs growing their own is that the crops can arrive in the kitchen untrimmed, allowing stocks to be made from skins and tops, or chefs can experiment with roots, leaves and flowers.

Over the years in which Jo has supplied planting plans, the team at The Star Inn – most notably Mike, the handyman, and Tina, who works in the hotel – have followed them faithfully. This gives Jo an enormous sense of pride, and she is delighted that the kitchen garden has proved to be such a success.

BELOW LEFT In addition to the main beds, Jo created a number of smaller ones for edible flowers and herbs.
BELOW RIGHT Cut flowers are grown to decorate the restaurant as well as to attract pollinating insects.

FRENCH BEANS

To add height and structure to the potager, Jo has included climbing varieties of French beans, which are supported up criss-cross bamboo canes or trellis. Meanwhile dwarf varieties are also planted, and these have the added advantage that they can be grown under cloches if the soil is cold or if temperatures cool at the start of the season.

The French beans are grown for their edible pods, picked when young and tender. There are varieties of yellow-podded, green-podded and purple-podded dwarf French bean (such as 'Purple Teepee'), so if your space is limited perhaps it might be a good idea to opt for the unusual yellow and purple beans. Blanch the the pods quickly and stop the cooking process by immersing them in cold water, so that they retain their colour. Some varieties of French beans are useful as they can be left on the plant longer and used as flageolet beans, when they are shelled and eaten like peas, or dried and used as haricot beans. Why not try varieties such as 'Canellino', 'Soissons' (flageolet beans), 'Barlotta' (borlotti beans) and 'Brown Dutch'?

French beans are half-hardy annuals and frost tender, so Jo recommends waiting for the soil to reach about 13°C/55°F before sowing direct outdoors. Climbing French beans require tying in until they find their own way up their supports, whether these be trellis, bamboo canes or hazel poles, 2.5m/8ft or 3m/10ft tall. Despite being bushy, dwarf French beans still require some support to stop them falling over and to keep the beans off the soil once fruiting. When planting out or when you spot seedlings emerging from the ground, insert some twiggy supports of beech or hazel for the beans to grow through; otherwise use canes and twine.

Be careful when watering French beans, particularly on hot sunny days, because the leaves will scorch and damage.

Beans fix nitrogen with their roots, which is good for the soil, so at the end of the season dig the roots back into the ground to help next season's crop as part of the seasonal rotation of vegetables.

FRENCH BEAN CALENDAR

SOW If you want to get a head start to the season, sow climbing French beans in root-trainers in a polytunnel or glasshouse and plant out only once there is little risk of frost, or have horticultural fleece on standby to protect young plants. Dwarf French beans can be started inside in pots and planted out after the danger of frost has passed.

Sow seeds generously in the ground, in single rows or double rows, then cover with fleece to help germination and also to protect young seedlings from wood pigeons.

CARE Water French beans well, especially when in flower, to help them set and produce the pods.

HARVEST Pods are ready for harvesting when they snap easily and before the beans can be seen through the pod. Pick dwarf varieties more gently than their climbing cousins – you can easily pull the plant out of the soil, so Jo recommends holding just behind the point at which the bean is attached to the plant, as well as the bean itself, so you have more control while pulling them off (see left).

WHITBY LOBSTER WITH QUAIL EGGS & GARDEN BEANS

SERVES 2

The Niçoise-style lobster dish is simply 'summer on a plate'; it is a real spectacle of rich summer colours and uses salad leaves and edible flowers from The Star Inn's kitchen garden, as well as vibrant mixed beans, so the flavours are all wonderfully fresh.

METHOD

1   Preheat the oven to 160°C/325°F/ gas mark 3. Cook the lobster in boiling water for 12 minutes, then split in half. Clean and prepare it by removing the tail meat and cutting it into 5 or so thin slices, then reposition in the tail shell, so that the red side of the flesh shows.

2   Cook the potatoes, quails' eggs and mixed beans in separate pans of salted boiling water for 12–15 minutes, 2 minutes and 1 minute, respectively, then refresh in iced, or at least very cold, water. Drain well and season the beans with salt and drizzle with olive oil. Remove the shells from the eggs.

3   Place the tomatoes on a baking sheet, drizzle with a little olive oil and sprinkle with salt. Then roast them for 1 hour. Remove from the oven and allow to cool, to intensify the flavour.

4   **To serve**, place half the beans and the potatoes on each plate with half the lobster tail. Arrange the tomatoes around each plate. Garnish with anchovies, garden herbs, quails' eggs and dots of garlic mayonnaise in a few of the gaps.

INGREDIENTS

450–500g/1–1.1lb native lobster
4 small new potatoes, halved
6 quails' eggs
150g/5oz mixed beans, topped and tailed
Rock salt
2 tsp olive oil
10 cherry tomatoes

TO SERVE
80g/2¹/₂oz marinaded anchovies
Mixed garden herbs, to garnish
30g/1oz aioli/garlic mayonnaise

HERITAGE APPLES

Because Andrew is dedicated to Yorkshire produce and suppliers, it was good to support this theme in the garden. Jo therefore bought heritage Yorkshire apple varieties for The Star Inn, especially 'Hunt House', as that is where Andrew grew up. She had to get her order in as early as possible – in spring for a bare-root winter delivery – as stock can be limited of any unusual or heritage variety. She planted them in well-drained soil in a sunny but sheltered site and then trained them as stepovers, cordons and espaliers, so they provided structure to the potager, dividing it up and giving it height. When correctly pruned, such apple trees can be compact as well as productive.

APPLE CALENDAR

PLANT Plant bare-root trees when dormant, from late autumn to early spring, while container-grown trees can be put in at any time of year. Dig a planting hole the same depth as the roots, but about three times the width of the root system. When backfilling the hole, make sure there is soil all around the roots and gently firm the top.
CARE Water well, and each spring feed with a general fertilizer.
HARVEST Apples are ripe and ready to use if they come away from the tree with just a gentle twist. The best method of storing apples is to wrap individual ones in newspaper and lay them on slatted trays, so air can circulate. Make sure the fruits are not touching, and remove any rotten ones.

JO & ANDREW'S
KITCHEN GARDEN SECRETS

- **Plant companions**: Beneficial planting combinations such as marigolds with tomatoes and nasturtiums with cabbages promote growth, encourage predators and pollinators, and deter pests. This practice also adds an ornamental touch to the edible garden.
- **Grow seasonally**: Although it may be tempting to try sowing or planting a bit too early or late in the season, your efforts are most likely to result in disappointment.
- **Plant visually**: When planning a planting schedule to form a tapestry of colours and combinations always consider the colours and textures of leaves, plant habits and flower and seed shapes.
- **Sow successionally**: With most crops you can ensure continuity of supply through the season by sowing at regular intervals.

GRANDPA
BUXTON

ROAST GROUSE WITH APPLE PURÉE & BRAMBLES

SERVES 4

If the Niçoise-style lobster dish is a celebration of full summer, Andrew's grouse recipe points towards the end of summer and early autumn – the 'season of mellow fruitfulness'. Apples and brambles (or blackberries) are a long-established combination, but by serving them separately you get the full impact of the individual fruits.

METHOD

1   Preheat the oven to 180°C/350°F/gas mark 4. Place all 4 grouse in an roasting tin, season with salt and pepper, then cover each bird's breast with a pancetta slice, to keep it moist, and roast for 16–18 minutes. Then remove from the oven and leave to rest.

2   **For the Ampleforth Abbey purée**, place the apples into a small saucepan, add a little water and the sugar, then bring to boil and cook until very soft. Purée in the food processor until smooth.

3   **For the mulled brambles**, bring the mulled wine to the boil. Then place the brambles in a small dish and cover with the hot wine. Leave to cool so the brambles can take on the flavours of the wine.

4   **For the sloe gin sauce**, heat the veal stock and reduce by half. At this point, add the sloe gin, which will give a rich and fruity flavour to the sauce.

5   **To serve**, take the breasts and legs off the grouse and keep warm. Spoon the Ampleforth Abbey purée on to each plate and place a breast and 2 legs on each plate, on top of a pancetta slice. Place the mulled brambles around each plate and finish with the sloe gin sauce, adding watercress on top, to garnish.

INGREDIENTS

4 young grouse, oven-ready
Salt and pepper
4 slices of pancetta
Watercress, to garnish

AMPLEFORTH ABBEY PURÉE
3 cooking apples, peeled, cored and quartered
100g/3^1/$_2$oz caster sugar

MULLED BRAMBLES
100ml/3^1/$_2$fl oz mulled wine
100g/3^1/$_2$oz brambles

SLOE GIN SAUCE
100ml/3^1/$_2$fl oz veal stock
50ml/2fl oz sloe gin

9

RIVER COTTAGE
Devon

Since first entering the nation's consciousness in 1998, River Cottage has come to stand for the importance of using the finest-quality, local produce in the right season. Hugh Fearnley-Whittingstall has inspired a generation to think about where their food comes from as well as shown exciting ways to use it. His team at River Cottage share this passion, and the kitchens and demonstration classrooms at Park Farm, the Devon-based headquarters, are a constant hive of activity. The vegetable garden located in front of the familiar, seventeenth-century, white farmhouse is no exception. Possibly one of the most visited productive plots in the UK, it also has to contend with the demands of filming Hugh's television series as well as supplying the kitchen with produce. This means vegetables might grow bigger than the chefs would prefer or sowings can be delayed, resulting in a late harvest. It is a fine balance for head gardener Craig Rudman and head chef Gill Meller, and their close working relationship smoothes the way and makes for an amazingly bountiful garden and inspirational recipes.

As a chef Gill has always believed in an ethical approach to food – his first job was at the organic travelling festival café, Henry's Beard. His passion about provenance has increased over the last ten years at River Cottage, as a result of meeting and working with so many food experts and having access to the very best produce. Along with his brigade, which fluctuates in number between eight and ten chefs depending on the season, Gill oversees the busy kitchen at headquarters: they serve sixty covers in winter and ninety in the summer months, when they can put tables outside. In addition to the evening service, they also produce food for River Cottage events, festivals, weddings and courses.

EXCEPTIONAL OUTPUT

The kitchen garden supplies 60 per cent of the produce in high season, which is an impressive amount, not least because the thin layer of soil is on top of Devon flint. Being in a valley, the garden has its own microclimate too: the temperature is slow to warm up in spring and, on occasion, a fog sits in the garden for a few days at a time, and it can get very wet at the end of the growing season.

For head gardener Craig, who is Kew-trained and grew up helping his father on his allotment, the setback of poor soil is easily overcome with a generous application of organic matter and working a crop rotation system. The 'Legume', 'Roots' and 'Alliums' beds have a huge amount of green waste added to the soil too. Craig is able to make a small amount of his own compost, but much of the green waste produced on the farm goes to the pigs, so most

The grower,
Craig Rudman

The chef,
Gill Meller

OPPOSITE The spectacular setting for River Cottage is well appreciated by visitors as well as those who see it on television.

organic matter is bought in from local authority green waste – as much as 14 tonnes at any one time, to serve these three beds and the polytunnel. The 'Brassicas' and 'Others' beds get well-rotted donkey manure from the donkey sanctuary just down the road. The microclimate and weather can be harder to overcome, but a variety of polytunnels, which extend the seasons and help provide a year-round supply of herbs and salad leaves, as well as choosing the right crop varieties go a long way to solving the problem conditions.

Craig sows shallots, onions, parsnips, chard, beetroot, broad beans, peas and baby salads in deep cells in the polytunnel in early spring. By mid-spring he can direct sow these varieties outdoors, to stagger the harvests. Craig also is keen to experiment with more exotic varieties such as oca, a beautifully pink-coloured tuber from South America, which is like a potato and has a magnificent citrus flavour. Oca leaves can be used in salads and as a garnish too. He also grows hardy gingers (*Zingiber*) and geraniums

(*Pelargonium*) and cardamom (*Elettaria cardamomum*) for their intoxicatingly fragrant leaves.

First-early potatoes are a must in Craig's kitchen garden – they are quick to mature and the flavour is unbeatable. Floury maincrops are not worthwhile, as they take up precious space and are bland in comparison to the first earlies. Blight is another reason to avoid later varieties, though in 2012 Park Farm had blight for the first time on the early potatoes, as a result of the prolonged period of wet weather. Craig recognizes that changing weather patterns and extreme seasons make it hard for first-time growers, but he is keen to get the message across that, even if the seasons conspire against you, it is always worth trying again the following year.

FROM PLOT TO PLATE

The productive garden is just across the farmyard from the kitchens at River Cottage, so it is easy for Gill and his chefs to discuss ideas about ingredients and developing dishes with Craig and his deputy, Will Livingstone; the chefs are always popping in and out of the garden on a regular basis. This works the other way around too. When Craig or Will deliver freshly harvested food direct to the kitchen

BELOW LEFT River Cottage HQ, a 25-hectare/60-acre farm, is located on the borders between Devon and Dorset.
BELOW RIGHT French beans produce a great yield so Gill's kitchen can enjoy fresh harvests throughout summer.

door, they have the opportunity to get plenty of useful feedback about particular varieties and types of produce.

As River Cottage is the headquarters of the whole business, there are weekly operations meetings to discuss in detail what can be sown or harvested. Oriental winter salads – mizuna (for example, 'Red Knight'), mibuna and mustards (for example, 'Green in Snow') – are favourites along with winter-hardy lettuces, fennel, parsley, coriander and red Russian kale and chard. Craig prefers to grow red Russian kale and chard in the polytunnel as well as outdoors, as he finds the leaves are more tender when protected against the elements, and they produce a bigger, long-lasting crop. All are extremely useful for Gill and his kitchen during the winter months.

As you would expect, there is plenty of experimentation too, and Craig and the resident forager, John Wright, have an ongoing discussion about the superiority of wild versus hybrid varieties: in John's opinion members of the goosefoot family such as fat hen (*Chenopodium album*) are better than cultivated spinach, and garden-grown seakale (*Crambe maritima*) is not a patch on the crop that is found on the dunes.

He is planning to graft more than fifty local heritage apple varieties on to 'M27' rootstocks, to train as stepovers around the edge of the kitchen garden. He would also like to increase the size of the garden and growing areas so he can produce the quantities required for the courses, dinners, weddings and festivals that are a year-round feature at River Cottage headquarters.

PERFECT PEAS

Peas are one of the ideal crops for growing in a restaurant's kitchen garden: when picked and then cooked in a matter of minutes, before the sugars turn to starch, they taste utterly delicious. Craig grows beautiful purple 'Ezeta's Krombek Blauwschokker' mangetout for both looks and taste. For River Cottage, a bed of peas is also an opportunity to make an attractive feature in an otherwise barren time for the garden. Thus they are ideal when your garden is visited and even filmed year-round.

PEA CALENDAR

SOW To provide delicious pods in late spring or early summer, Craig starts his peas off in the polytunnel in late winter. Successive sowings of second earlies and maincrop varieties will provide peas until mid-autumn. To sow outdoors, he waits until the soil has warmed.

CARE He plants out in early or mid-spring in trenches, 5cm/2in deep and 7cm/3in apart. Craig waters regularly when they flower and adds a layer of mulch to help keep the soil moist.

HARVEST For the most succulent flavoursome peas, Craig harvests daily when the pods are filled.

Craig harvests hazels from the farm on the hillside. These make great supports, which last the season. Rather than trimming off the wispy shoots, he twines them together to create beautiful flowing arching shapes. Although more time-consuming than just plunging hazel sticks in the ground, it is worth the effort as the ground is pretty bare in early to mid-spring, when peas are planted in soil. Birds can be a problem, so he protects seedlings with mesh when they are first planted out. During the growing season Craig keeps the pea plants well watered.

PEAS WITH HAM & CHEESE

SERVES 2–3 AS A STARTER

INGREDIENTS

LABNEH
1 litre/1 ¾ pints plain, whole milk yogurt
1 tsp fine sea salt

TO SERVE
Handfuls of podded garden peas
8 slices of good-quality, air-dried ham
Handful of tender pea tops, plus any with nice flowers
12–16 small mint leaves
A few small nasturtium leaves
Extra-virgin olive oil
Salt and pepper
Toasted sourdough bread

Freshly picked peas are one of the vegetable garden's true gifts. When young and tender, such peas do not need cooking. At River Cottage, Gill likes to place bowls of peas in the pod down the supper tables, carefully arranged next to bowls of salty pork crackling. This is more of an assembly than a recipe. A few simple foods – such as peas and ham; mint and peas; ham and cheese – go beautifully well together. Gill accompanies such delights with light salad enhanced by a spoonful of rich home-made labneh – a fresh cheese made with natural yogurt.

METHOD

1 **For the labneh**, put the yogurt in a bowl, add the salt and mix well. Line a sieve with a square of scalded muslin or a thin cotton cloth, and place it over a bowl. Spoon the yogurt into the muslin, then flip the sides over the yogurt to enclose it. Transfer to the refrigerator and leave for at least 24 hours and up to two or three days. Lots of liquid will drain into the bowl, but you need to turn the yogurt over in the sieve every so often, to encourage it to do this evenly. Eventually the yogurt should end up looking like a soft cheese.

2 **To serve**, add the peas to a small saucepan of lightly salted boiling water and cook for 1–2 minutes, until just tender. Drain, and refresh in iced water to stop the cooking process and help to keep the pea colour. Divide the slices of ham between four plates, followed by a spoonful of labneh. Scatter over the peas, their tops and flowers, the mint and nasturtium leaves. Trickle with good olive oil. Season and serve with toasted sourdough bread.

CRAIG & GILL'S
KITCHEN GARDEN SECRETS

- **Perfect soil**: To grow plants successfully you must look after your soil. For most plants in the veg patch, aim towards the holy grail of a free-draining, moisture-retentive soil of pH 6.5–7.0.
- **Water sparingly**: Do this only when absolutely necessary! If needed, water very heavily but infrequently.
- **Grow hard**: By providing little extra water or nutrition, plants are able to withstand pests and diseases better than soft pampered ones. Make the soil and the plants do the work.
- **Avoid forcing**: Grow plants when they want to do so. Plants will experience stress if forced to grow when conditions are not optimal, leading to pest and disease problems as well as bolting.
- **Take stock**: View the garden, plants, soil and the animals within it as an interconnected ecosystem. Learn the life cycles of your plants, about beneficial insects and pests and discover how to grow well in an environmentally responsible way. Continually learn from your successes and mistakes, and understand that this knowledge is a lifelong evolution.

ROSE GERANIUM CUTTINGS

For the River Cottage chefs, rose geranium (*Pelargonium graveolens*) is a very useful plant as its lemon-rose-scented leaves make a delicious stock syrup when boiled in sugary water. To secure a steady supply of the leaves for the kitchen, Craig takes softwood stem-tip cuttings from this tender perennial in spring or he uses semi-ripe cuttings, which are less prone to rotting, in early summer. These are cut from a non-flowering shoot, just above a bud on the parent plant, and are 10cm/4in long. He prepares each shoot by slicing below a leaf node so it is 8cm/3¼in long, then removing the lower leaves and pinching out the growing tip. He then fills a small pot with compost and using a dibber makes holes for the cuttings. Having been watered well, the pot is placed in a heated propagator set at 18–24°C/64–75°F or covered with a plastic bag and put in a warm spot. Once rooted, after about ten weeks, the young plants are hardened off outside and potted on individually.

LEFT and BELOW To propagate a rose geranium plant, cut from a non-flowering shoot, just above a bud (1). Make a clean slice just below a leaf node so the shoot is about 8cm/3¼in long (2). Remove the lower leaves and pinch out the growing tip, then leave in water while preparing the other cuttings (3). Use a dibber such as a pencil to make a hole in the potting compost and insert the cutting (4), then gently firm in with the pencil and water well.

ROSE GERANIUM PANNA COTTA & BLACKCURRANT SORBET

SERVES 6–8

In this gorgeous, fragrant and delicate pudding, the panna cotta is infused with rose geranium. This has highly scented leaves with a unique and beautiful flavour, and they are often used to perfume sugars, ice creams, cakes, jams and syrups.

INGREDIENTS

PANNA COTTA
6–8 rose geranium leaves
200ml/^{1}/$_3$ pint milk
500ml/17^1/$_2$fl oz double cream
60g/2oz caster sugar
Enough leaf gelatine to set 500ml/17^1/$_2$fl oz of liquid
300ml/^{1}/$_2$ pint plain, whole-milk yogurt

SORBET
175g/6oz granulated sugar
225ml/8fl oz water
Sprig of thyme
500ml/17^1/$_2$fl oz blackcurrants, topped and tailed

TO SERVE
Rose geranium sugar, to decorate

METHOD

1 **For the panna cotta**, roughly tear the geranium leaves into a saucepan. Add the milk, cream and sugar and bring to a simmer, stirring to dissolve the sugar and help infuse the cream. Remove from the heat. Meanwhile, calculate how many gelatine leaves you need to set 500ml/17^1/$_2$fl oz liquid. Put them in a bowl of cold water to soak for about 5 minutes, to soften. Squeeze out excess water, then add the soaked gelatine to the hot infused cream and stir gently until dissolved. When the mixture has cooled slightly, stir in the yogurt. Pass the mixture through a sieve into a clean jug. Pour the panna cotta mix into the dariole moulds (cylindrical cooking moulds) and put in the refrigerator for at least 4 hours, to set.

2 **For the sorbet**, put the sugar in a saucepan with the water and the thyme. Heat gently, stirring, until the sugar has dissolved, then add the blackcurrants and bring just to a simmer. Cook gently for 5–10 minutes, stirring occasionally, until the blackcurrants are soft. Pass the fruit and liquid through a fine sieve into a clean bowl, pressing the fruit in the sieve with the back of a spoon, to extract a maximum amount of juice. Chill the mixture. When it is cold, churn it in an ice cream machine until you have a vivid purple, soft-set sorbet. Then transfer the mixture to a freezer container and freeze until firm.

3 **To serve**, take the sorbet out of the freezer 20 minutes before you plan to eat it. To serve the panna cotta, dip the moulds in hot water very briefly to loosen. Carefully turn out each panna cotta on to a plate. Serve with a spoonful of sorbet and, if you like, a scattering of rose geranium sugar – for crunch.

JEKKA McVICAR & THE COMPANY OF COOKS

Gloucestershire

10

According to Jekka McVicar, herbs are always bouncing between being in and out of fashion and are currently enjoying a renaissance. Her recent collaboration with chefs at the Company of Cooks has helped to spread the message about their uses. Long may it continue.

Jekka, the 'Queen of Herbs', has organically grown more than 650 varieties of herbs on her farm near Bristol for the past twenty-seven years. During that time she has been awarded more than sixty gold medals at RHS flower shows, including fourteen at Chelsea and the RHS Lawrence Medal for best exhibit. She has written books, appeared on television and radio shows and is regarded by cooks and gardeners alike as the herb guru.

A recent decision to scale down her mail-order business encouraged Jekka to move away from the heavy clay soil of the farm on which she had grown her herbs. Instead, using a mix of compost, grit and an enriched biochar soil improver, she has created the optimum growing medium in sixteen raised beds. In a new school at the farm — her Herbetum —

she holds workshops and classes for schoolchildren as well as chefs who are looking to expand their knowledge and understanding of culinary herbs.

Given her wealth of experience about growing herbs, it is no surprise that chefs, including celebrities such as Jamie Oliver, Raymond Blanc and Nigel Slater, seek her out for inspiration and advice. Jekka is excited about educating chefs, especially as she believes slow-grown, local and seasonal herbs taste better and are hardier and are likely to last longer than those grown overseas.

SAVOUR THE FLAVOUR

Among Jekka's more recent clientele is the Company of Cooks — a catering company for prestigious venues such as the Royal Opera House, the Imperial War Museum and RHS Garden Wisley. Each week it provides food for huge numbers of people: for example, it serves seven thousand main dishes during

OPPOSITE Jekka McVicar (holding a tray of herbs) loves to host chefs, such as Claire, Chris and Justin from The Company of Cooks, at her new Herbetum.

The grower,
Jekka McVicar

Culinary director,
Claire Clark

Chef,
Chris Handley

Chef,
Justin Hammett

the first week of early spring; and ten thousand dishes during the first week of early summer. Despite the large-scale numbers, the Company of Cooks considers seasonality and quality of produce to be the starting point for its menus. This is unusual in the mass-catering sector, which normally regards profit as the main priority. When it comes to sourcing ingredients, the Company of Cooks is setting a high standard within their industry, and it emphasizes British producers using native varieties. Despite the challenge of the nationwide spread of its clients, the Company of Cooks chooses local produce if possible. Its reach however can be just that bit farther than a single restaurant: it sources its rhubarb from the 'rhubarb triangle' in North Yorkshire, strawberries from Kent, apples from Wisley and of course herbs from Jekka in Bristol.

HERBS ON THE MENU

The culinary director of the Company of Cooks is Claire Clark MBE, former head pastry chef at Thomas

BELOW Jekka now grows her herb collection in raised beds so that she can provide the appropriate growing medium.

Keller's French Laundry in California and part of the launch team for the Wolseley in London. She recently led the team to develop menus inspired by the growing calendar at RHS Garden Wisley. They trialled desserts and bakery items such as strawberry granita with basil and borage flower, lavender shortbread and honey-lavender crème brûlée.

Together with Royal Opera House chefs Chris Handley and Justin Hammett, Claire visits Jekka to discuss and taste specific herb varieties and to discover new flavours. For Chris and Justin, the Royal Opera House is a theatre and the ingredients, food and service must 'sing' – as if in their own opera. For Claire, it is a chance to be more adventurous with herbs not only professionally but also when using herbs from her patio at home, where she grows different thymes, fennel, parsley, chives and rosemary. She loves combining these flavours with pastry and uses them to create savoury desserts – another popular trend thanks to the perception that they are more healthy than sweet desserts.

Such is the enthusiasm of these three chefs that in 2013 they were part of a team involved in making a herb garden on the alfresco terrace of the Royal Opera House's Amphitheatre Restaurant. They also helped start Herbfest, part of the summer-long Festival of Neighbourhood partnered by the Eden Project, which took place at London's Southbank Centre. While the main festival spread a more general message about urban growing, the intention behind Herbfest was to enthuse people about this particular group of plants. The Royal Opera House, Southbank Centre, Kenwood House, RHS Garden Wisley and The Garden Café at Regent's Park were transformed with large herb installations and miniature gardens. In the greenhouses on the Southbank they used bay, chives, fennel, French tarragon, lavender, lemon verbena, oregano, parsley, rosemary, sage, savoury, spearmint and thyme – their idea being to encourage people to grow their own herbs.

Chris, Justin and Claire also designed menus to show how varied and versatile herbs can be, whether picked fresh and eaten raw, crumbled with salt to make a rub or ground into a pesto.

WINTER SAVOURY

Jekka grows all her herbs in raised beds, with well-drained soil, and she resists the urge to feed them as herbs prefer poor soil. They also cope well in containers, given a mix of a soil-based compost and coarse horticultural grit and a warm sunny spot. However she finds winter savoury (*Satureja montana*) is also a useful herb in the vegetable plot, because it retains some leaves during winter and she can harvest these to enliven soups and stews. Winter savoury also has soothing properties if you crush its leaves and rub them on a wasp or bee sting.

To ensure that she always has young vigorous plants Jekka regularly propagates winter savoury from cuttings. She recommends taking the cuttings in the early morning and putting the young shoots in a plastic bag, which has been misted with water, to keep them fresh. She removes the lower leaves from each stem, using sharp secateurs rather than pulling them off by hand, to reduce the risk of tearing the stems and causing infection. Jekka makes a cut just beneath the third or fourth leaf node and pushes the

WINTER SAVOURY CALENDAR

SOW Jekka starts off winter savoury seeds in a polytunnel in early spring. They need some heat to germinate so she places them in a propagator at a temperature of 20°C/68°F.

CARE Seedlings are prone to damping off so she does not overwater. When large enough, she transplants them into their final growing positions. If the plants are pot-grown, Jekka applies a weekly feed during the growing season – a comfrey or seaweed tea is ideal.

HARVEST Winter savoury is best harvested from early spring to late autumn, and for the strongest flavour she picks new growth. Picking top growth also helps prolong a good supply of leaves. Jekka also gathers the small tasty flowers to eat.

shoot into a compost-filled cell of a modular tray. Having sprayed the cuttings with water, she covers the modular tray with plastic or a lid. When she can see roots appearing from the bottom of the tray, she pots on the young plants and keeps them in a cold frame until the following spring, when they can be planted out in their final positions.

CHARCOAL-COOKED LAMB RACK WITH SAVOURY POTATOES

JUSTIN HAMMETT

SERVES 4

Justin loves the flavour of winter savoury – it is the unsung hero of the herb garden and tastes like a cross between thyme and rosemary with just a hint of fennel. Coming across winter savoury at Jekka's farm reminded him of a visit to Malta, in 2003, where this herb is a favourite addition to potatoes, lamb and tomatoes, in home kitchens and restaurants alike.

METHOD

1 Preheat the oven to 200°C/400°F/gas mark 6. Heat 3 pieces of wood charcoal, each 4cm/1½in long, over a gas flame until they glow red. Create a cup shape from a square of tinfoil and leave on one side. Season the lamb racks with salt and pepper. Heat the oil in a sturdy, cast-iron casserole and seal the lamb, fat-side down. Drain off any excess oil. Put the tinfoil cup into the casserole alongside the racks, and, using tongs, carefully place the glowing charcoal pieces in it. Put the lid on the casserole and place in the oven for 20 minutes. The juices of the lamb should run pink when pierced with a skewer. Leave to rest for about 20 minutes before carving into cutlets. Discard the charcoal and skim any fat from the surface of any juices left in the pan.

2 **For the red wine jus,** simmer the stock with the red wine and herbs until syrupy and thickened. Add any charcoal-infused juices from the lamb to the jus. Strain and discard the herbs.

3 **For the savoury potatoes,** preheat the oven to 180°C/350°F/gas mark 4. Brush the bottom and sides of a shallow ovenproof glass dish or small roasting tin with olive oil. Arrange some potatoes in a single overlapping layer in a concentric circle over the base of the dish or tin. Scatter with one-third of the onions and a sprinkling of winter savoury leaves, season with salt and pepper, add one-third of the cherry tomatoes and generously

INGREDIENTS

2 racks of lamb (6 bones in each)
Salt and pepper
4 tsp extra-virgin olive oil
Edible flowers, to garnish (optional)

RED WINE JUS
750ml/1⅓ pints chicken stock
375ml/⅔ pint red wine
Sprig of mint
Small sprig of rosemary

SAVOURY POTATOES
120ml/4½fl oz extra-virgin olive oil, plus some for coating ovenproof dish
1.2kg/2½lb potatoes, 'Desirée' or 'King Edward', peeled and thinly sliced
250g/9oz onions, thinly sliced
4 sprigs of winter savoury
Salt and pepper
500g/1lb 1oz cherry tomatoes

ROASTED VINE TOMATOES
6–7 cherry tomatoes, on the vine
2 tsp extra-virgin olive oil
Sprig of winter savoury

drizzle with 40ml/1½fl oz olive oil. Repeat this process three times, finishing with the onions, savoury and tomatoes on top. Season and drizzle with the remaining olive oil. Bake for 45–50 minutes, until the tomato skins have darkened and the potatoes are tender. Remove from the oven; leave to cool for a few minutes.

4 **For the roasted vine tomatoes,** turn the oven up to 200°C/400°F/gas mark 6. Put the tomato vine in a small roasting tin, drizzle with oil and sprinkle with winter savoury leaves. Roast for about 10 minutes, until the skins have blistered and the tomatoes softened.

5 **To serve,** place the roasted vine tomatoes over the savoury potatoes before serving with the lamb and red wine jus. Garnish with edible flowers.

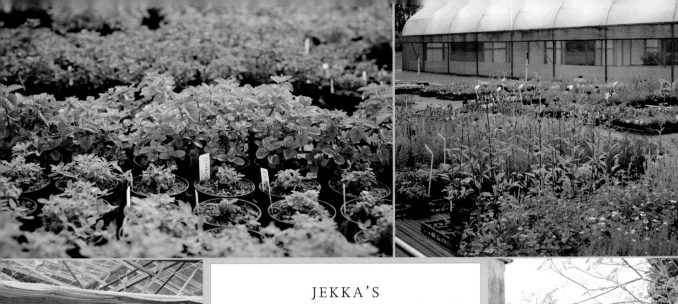

JEKKA'S
KITCHEN GARDEN SECRETS

- **Play safe**: Use seed compost for container sowing – potting or multipurpose compost is too rich in nutrients, and makes the seedlings develop too fast.
- **Water first**: Always water your seed trays and modules before sowing, allowing the water to soak through and completely moisten the compost.
- **Start small**: Plant just a few herbs that you are going to use in the kitchen. This way you will be able to maintain them and harvest them regularly. In turn this will keep the plants under control and stop them rampaging through your garden.
- **Cut back**: Trim thyme, sage, lavender, mint, oregano, hyssop and savoury after flowering to encourage the plants to put on new growth for late season pickings. It also helps to protect the plants from heavy rain, gales and snow.

FENNEL FLOWERS

These flowers have a delicate aniseed flavour and are slightly crunchy, while fennel seeds and its feathery foliage are delicious too. Jekka suggests planting fennel away from dill, as they may cross-pollinate, while nearby coriander plants can affect the flavour of the fennel. She grows fennel in well-drained, fertile soil and cuts it back as part of regular maintenance. However she leaves the seed heads over the winter to self-sow and bulk up her stocks as well as to give birds a treat.

TASTY THYME

There is a wide range of thyme flavours to choose from, so it is worth researching which ones are most likely to appeal. For easy pickings, Jekka recommends the upright varieties such as *Thymus* 'Silver Queen', T. 'Fragrantissimus' or T. *vulgaris* 'Compactus'.

As with winter savoury (see page 95), Jekka takes softwood cuttings of thyme and overwinters them in a cold frame. Thyme can also be divided, by lifting the plant and splitting it in two in spring. In hot dry climates you can divide in autumn too.

GRILLED MACKEREL WITH BEETROOT
CHRIS HANDLEY

SERVES 4 AS A STARTER

No part of the herbs in Jekka's fabulous gardens are wasted — from flowers to stems, leaves and even the pollen — all feature in Chris's cooking. He is a fan of using her herbs to complement and contrast with the flavours of other seasonal ingredients, and he believes that such great produce does not need much done to it to create a memorable dish. Grilled mackerel makes a striking partnership with sweet beetroot and the aromatic, aniseed-like notes of fennel tops. Fennel pollen, found in the tiny dried heads of fennel flowers, has a splendidly sweet and intense character — and is also a great match for mackerel.

INGREDIENTS

100g/3^1/$_2$oz candy-striped beetroot
100g/3^1/$_2$oz golden beetroot
100g/3^1/$_2$oz red beetroot
2 tbsp sherry vinegar
6 tbsp lemon oil
4 mackerel fillets, in 3cm/1^1/$_4$in wide slices
Salt and pepper
2 tsp extra-virgin olive oil

TO SERVE
Fennel tops
1 tsp fennel pollen, to garnish
Bergamot flowers, to garnish

METHOD

1   Dice half the raw beetroot. Bring 3 small saucepans of salted water to the boil and add each beetroot variety to a separate saucepan. Return the water to the boil and after 5 seconds drain the beetroot and leave on one side. Whisk the vinegar with the lemon oil and stir it into the diced beetroot, to marinate. Finely slice the remaining beetroot on a mandolin or use a sharp knife to cut them into wafer-thin rounds. Sprinkle the mackerel slices with salt and pepper, and brush with olive oil. Cook, skin-side facing upwards, under a very hot grill for 3 minutes on one side only — until crisp.

2   **To serve**, put some fennel tops on each plate and then fold the beetroot slices in half and arrange around the fronds. Add a mackerel piece to each plate skin-side facing upwards, and scatter with the marinated diced beetroot. Drizzle around the marinated beetroot dressing. Sprinkle fennel pollen over the fish, and finish with more fennel tops and bergamot flowers.

THE RIVER CAFÉ

London

Ruth Rogers's and the late Rose Gray's restaurant, The River Café, is one of the UK's most celebrated eateries. Having started life in 1987, it quickly evolved into one of the most dynamic, exciting restaurants of its day and still remains influential twenty-six years on. Not only were Rose and Ruth pioneers in a male-dominated industry, but they were also thinking about seasonality when very few other chefs were doing so.

It is widely acknowledged that Rose and Ruth introduced cavolo nero and rocket to the UK market, bringing seeds back from one of their Italian trips and using them in their recipes. These foods, which are now staples in most vegetable plots, inspired other chefs and growers to search for something a little different.

Some of our most well-known chefs, including Hugh Fearnley-Whittingstall, Jamie Oliver, Sam Clark, Stevie Parle and April Bloomfield, worked at The River Café, and each found it to be a truly inspirational experience that shaped how they viewed ingredients and approached cooking in their individual careers. Evidently Rose's and Ruth's enthusiasm for the best and freshest produce, their style and their ability to create a family atmosphere at work, set them apart.

In Ruth's own words, the garden is crucial to The River Café, and this is as much about its fresh produce and seasonality as it is about creating an aesthetically pleasing environment in which customers can enjoy alfresco dinners. It is also an important place for the staff to relax and enjoy.

OPPOSITE Simon and Ruth carefully select the variety of produce they will grow in their compact container garden.
BELOW Cut-and-come-again crops such as sorrel grow well in containers, but will need regular watering.

The grower,
Simon Hewitt

The chef,
Ruth Rogers

Ruth and Rose created the garden soon after starting the restaurant. Rose's grandfather, Sir Trevor Lawrence, was a former president of the RHS, and she herself was a keen gardener. The idea of growing vegetables, herbs and fruit for the restaurant seemed a natural progression to Rose and tied in well with both of the women's vision for The River Café. Ruth describes Rose as a brave courageous gardener who liked to push the boundaries, discovering new varieties on road trips and bringing a bewildering variety of seeds back to grow herself. Ruth, along with many other chefs and growers, found this inspiring. While Ruth loves to come out to the garden to find out what is in season and what is ready, it was Rose who was the passionate grower.

The garden is now managed by Kew-trained Simon Hewitt, who joined the team in 2008. He is a real foodie who loves to grow fruit and vegetables – an essential value for the only gardener at The River Café. Simon adored working with Rose as

one gardener to another, but he finds Ruth exciting because she approaches the crops from a chef's perspective – she considers all parts of the plant, from shoot to root, as potential ingredients.

He grows his crops in containers in order to make the most of limited space and from an aesthetic viewpoint. Annual vegetables and salad leaves can happily thrive in pots as well as perennial crops and larger specimens such as mulberries, quinces and figs. The large, iroko-teak-clad, marine-ply containers have coasters attached to the bottoms, so Simon can move them around to enjoy the best growing positions during the year. This flexibility also solved the problem of ripe juicy fruits dropping on customers when the trees were placed next to their tables. These days the laden, soft-fruit-bearing trees are wheeled out of harm's way, to the edge of the garden, until the summer is over.

Given the limitations of the garden space at The River Café, Simon chooses to grow crops that are hard to get hold of or are of particularly high value – pea shoots and courgette flowers are a must, for example. Other important produce for the kitchen is herbs – thyme, marjoram, basil and parsley. Crops

BELOW LEFT Figs are ideal fruit to grow in large pots and are an attractive addition to a container garden.
BELOW RIGHT Edible flowers such as nasturtiums are a great addition to The River Café's larder.

such as borlotti beans, Swiss chard, cavolo nero and tomatoes are useful too, helping to educate chefs and waiters about seasonality as well as being a living example to the customers of what they are eating.

TASTE TESTS

Because the container garden cannot supply enough produce for The River Café's 1,500 weekly covers, its role has evolved into producing a constant source of ideas for the kitchen. Simon, Ruth and the team try out new varieties too, to decide on crops to grow from season to season. For example, Simon nurtures seven varieties of tomatoes including 'Yellow Pear', 'Lilliput' and 'Rio Grande'. He prefers the small- and mid-sized fruits, because the smaller they are the better they taste in our climate. Without the help of a polytunnel or the guarantee of long hot summers, big tomatoes are not feasible, as they produce only a few fruits on each plant and they require a lot of sun to make them taste great. Simon is happy to keep to a core variety, mostly heritage varieties from northern Italy, as their colder temperate climate suits the UK's growing conditions very well.

Crops are planned six months ahead – from the initial selection of plants to ordering seeds. This allows Simon to have some seedlings growing at his home in case he needs to use them to plug gaps when seeds fail at The River Café, where there is no additional space nor a greenhouse.

The synergy between garden and kitchen is incredible at The River Café. Most of the staff work in the garden in their spare time – from the chefs to the team in the office – as Simon is on site only one day a week. Simon therefore relies on this input on the days he is not at the garden, especially when it comes to harvesting produce. The team take this one step farther too, as the waiters are expected to prepare the vegetables before each service. It connects them with the ingredients and allows them to talk knowledgeably and with confidence to customers. Simon has worked in the kitchen too and for him it is an invaluable experience, both working with produce he has grown and on a broader level.

At The River Café Ruth and Rose set out to create this connection between ingredient and the finished dish, and without doubt they have succeeded.

SORREL CALENDAR

SOW Sow into well-forked-through soil, in early spring or early autumn, then lightly cover over the sorrel's small seeds.
CARE Once germinated, thin to leave 5cm/2in bare soil between plants. Simon applies a slow-release, granular feed once in spring and again in midsummer.
HARVEST Sorrel is ready for harvest in around eight weeks and can be picked from spring to autumn. Simon and the team harvest with scissors, starting with the outermost leaves. Those too small for use are left in the centre and should be ready to gather two weeks later. If a plant bolts and goes to seed, it is cut back and encouraged to produce a final flush of growth.

LEAFY SORREL

This easy-to-raise crop is often used at The River Café in frittatas, soups and salads. Sorrel (*Rumex acetosa*) is best grown in shade, to stop the sun making the leaves tough and inedible. This requirement is useful for The River Café's garden, as much of it is in dappled shade during summer. Simon points out that sorrel leaves are easily mistaken for dock leaves, so always look closely before picking. Sorrel leaves are elongated and arrow-shaped and, unlike dock leaves, the young foliage has a sensational lemon flavour. The oldest and most productive sorrel bed in the garden is four years old. As this crop is so well loved by the kitchen during spring and summer, Simon now cultivates three beds of sorrel.

SORREL FRITTATA

SERVES 2

INGREDIENTS

Large handful of sorrel leaves, tough stalks
    removed
4 large, organic free-range eggs
Maldon sea salt and pepper
4 tbsp olive oil, plus some to drizzle
20g/³⁄₄oz butter
150g/5oz mascarpone cheese
50g/2oz Parmesan cheese, freshly grated

This frittata is a welcome addition to antipasti or on its own, and the sorrel in the recipe gives this dish a vibrant lemony flavour and is very fresh.

METHOD

1   Preheat the oven to 230°C/450°F/gas mark 8. Roughly chop the sorrel. Break the eggs into a bowl and lightly beat. Season the eggs with salt and pepper, then add half the sorrel. Heat the olive oil and butter in a medium-sized, ovenproof frying pan, tilting the pan to coat the surface. Add the egg mixture and, almost immediately, half the mascarpone, pushing the mascarpone into the thickening egg mixture with a wooden spoon.

2   When the frittata is almost set, add the remaining sorrel leaves and mascarpone. Scatter with 1 tbsp Parmesan and drizzle with a little olive oil. Season with salt and pepper and place in the oven for 1–2 minutes.

3   Remove from the oven when the frittata is crisp on the edges and slightly runny in the centre. Loosen the frittata from the pan, with a spatula, and serve on a warm plate. Scatter over the remaining Parmesan.

SIMON & RUTH'S
KITCHEN GARDEN SECRETS

- **Hazel tepees**: Train indeterminate tomatoes up hazel tepees, growing four plants against each tepee. Simon allows the first side shoot of each plant to grow, tying it against the main shoot. This way he gets eight productive shoots from four plants.
- **Container soil mix**: Soil in containers dries out far faster than a bed in the ground, so fill them with a mix of 80 per cent loam-based compost and 20 per cent garden compost. The loam retains water and nutrients for longer while the compost feeds the soil biosphere, aiding plant growth. Multipurpose compost can be an additional ingredient in your soil recipe.
- **Sun and shade**: Shade can often inhibit flowering in some plants, but it does not stop them trying to develop leaves. Therefore plant fruiting crops in the sun and place salad leaves in the shadier parts of your plot.
- **Sowing deadline**: Winter crops such as cavolo nero should be started in early summer. Sowing any later than midsummer is pointless as plants do not have time to reach a worthwhile size before the chills of autumn curtail their growth. Big cavolo nero plants in autumn will provide plenty of big healthy leaves for *ribollita* in winter.
- **Three crops from the same plant**: Sow autumn broad beans in late summer, so you can then harvest the tips of already sturdy plants for a warm, mid-autumn day's salad. The chefs at The River Café also serve the growing tips of broad beans in early summer, followed by the beans.

FIG CALENDAR

PLANT The ideal time to plant a fig tree is in spring, even though strictly speaking you can plant it at any time of the year if it is container-grown. Choose a pot one size bigger than its current one, and leave a 3cm/1¼in gap between the soil and the top of the pot, to make watering easier.

CARE In autumn remove anything bigger than a pea-sized fruitlet as only the smallest ones are likely to withstand the winter weather. Cover the plant with horticultural fleece if there is a risk of frost.

HARVEST Harvest figs from mid- to late summer. It is best to let the sun warm them to improve the flavour before eating them fresh from the tree.

BOUNTEOUS FIGS

To ensure a bountiful summer crop of delicious figs, Simon grows 'Brown Turkey' at The River Café. This variety is well suited to container growing as it likes to have its roots restricted, to encourage fruiting. It prefers a sunny position — against a wall is ideal — and protection from cold wet winter weather. Figs are happy in most soils, but ensure that they have good drainage. Simon uses John Innes No. 3 rather than multipurpose compost, buying it in tonne bags. He also prefers to apply blood, fish and bone fertilizer in spring, which breaks down over three months. During the growing season he applies a seaweed-based feed too.

Simon always wears gloves when handling the fig tree as its sap can irritate skin. To keep the fig healthy, he prunes it in early spring, to remove dead branches. Then, when it has started to put on growth by early summer, he removes the shoot tips of this new growth, leaving four to five leaves. Simon prunes the specimens at The River Café back to a height of 1.75m/6ft and removes three-year-old stems each year. He repots every second spring into fresh potting soil, and at the same time saws 5cm/2in off each side of the root ball.

FIG, MOZZARELLA & BASIL SALAD

SERVES 4

INGREDIENTS

6 ripe figs, green or purple
4 mozzarella balls
Salt and pepper
2 tbsp green basil
2 tbsp purple basil
Juice of 1 lemon
Extra-virgin olive oil

Figs and mozzarella are a classic River Café combination. The quality of the ingredients – ripe figs, fresh buffalo mozzarella and sweet green and purple basil – is the key to this dish.

METHOD

1   Cut off the top stem of each fig and cut each fig in half. Tear each mozzarella ball into four pieces. Place the figs and mozzarella pieces on individual serving plates. Season and scatter over the basil.
2   Mix the lemon juice with four times its volume of olive oil and season.
3   Pour the dressing over each plate and serve.

12

MONACHYLE MHOR HOTEL

Perthshire

You might expect to see locally reared, Balquhidder venison, beef, pork, lamb and game on the menu at Tom Lewis's boutique hotel, Monachyle Mhor, but the idea of Balquhidder-grown fennel and baby-leaf salads might raise an eyebrow or two. The short growing season combined with regularly cold temperatures are not the best conditions for such crops.

Monachyle Mhor is situated only an hour and a half's drive from Edinburgh and is set in Tom's 810-hectare/2,000-acre family farm in the Trossachs, which is regarded by most to be the 'highlands in miniature'. Two lochs – Voil and Doine – lap the edges of the 6.5-kilometre/4-mile track winding up to the hotel, and tree-covered, rocky outposts are silhouetted against the wild, heather-covered hills in the distance. You are likely to see hares and highland cattle before you catch sight of a dwelling.

It is a breathtakingly beautiful spot, but it can be a considerable challenge to cultivate vegetables in the shadow of these peaks. The site has extreme growing conditions according to the gardener, Alan MacInnes. Seasons start late and finish early, light levels can be low and pests tend to be bigger than the usual aphids and mites. But that is not to say gardening there is unsuccessful or demoralizing.

When Alan joined the team at Monachyle Mhor in early spring 2012, Tom's brief was for him to produce enough crops so that every dish served in the hotel would feature something from the kitchen garden. For Tom it is a question of giving his food a sense of provenance and identity as well as adding value for his guests. He is optimistic about the potential of the productive patch, not least because he and his wife, Lisa, and sister, Melanie, looked after it for several years until business demands proved too distracting.

Scottish weather aside, Tom and Alan's goal is achievable in the growing season but is somewhat ambitious for the winter months. Having overcome

OPPOSITE Although a chef, Tom grew vegetables at Monachyle Mhor for years and is a mine of information for Alan.
BELOW Truly breathtaking scenery of lochs and mountains surrounds this Scottish hotel.

The grower,
Alan MacInnes

The chef,
Tom Lewis

his first hurdles, such as preventing crops from being devoured by roaming deer and sheep, Alan is gradually getting to grips with the testing growing conditions. He aims to harvest three crops from one raised bed, possibly four in a good season, but then he must make provision for a smaller winter crop. Tom is happy for produce to be preserved – pickled, dried or even frozen. He feels chefs can be a little too precious about preserved food, and prefers to use his own frozen produce on a winter plate, grown 100 metres/110 yards away, rather than fresh produce flown in from overseas. However seasonality and locality are the ethos behind the choice of ingredients, and if food is not from the garden or the surrounding Trossachs then the aim is to source it from no farther than 50 kilometres/30 miles from Monachyle Mhor.

Choosing the right variety and quantity of a crop to grow for a kitchen was a new challenge for Alan, who trained at the Royal Botanic Garden Edinburgh. It is especially hard to assess quantities required

BELOW LEFT Tom and his family have run the hotel at Balquhidder for more than twenty years.
BELOW RIGHT Locally reared livestock is the source for some of the seasonal menus at Monachyle Mhor.

when you have not grown for chefs before. Alan was aware that just as you could harvest an entire bed for one evening's service you could find yourself with a glut too.

LISTENING TO THE SEASONS

Alan took his first year to observe and understand the kitchen's routine as well as the Balquhidder's season. Already he has witnessed a typically late start to the growing season with temperatures failing to stay consistently above 10°C/50°F until early summer. He also had to get to know the garden to understand the optimum position for particular crops.

Each of the eight raised beds has slightly different soil types, with some being quite heavy clay while others are more sandy. Alan had to establish which was which for crops such as runner beans (which prefer the sturdier clay) and salads (which cope with light, free-draining soil). He aims to change the soil profile in the beds and make them all more balanced by adding organic matter and growing green manures.

Turnips, or *navets*, have proven to be successful with the chefs, who like to use them when they are small

and have an intense flavour. As they are harvested quickly and do not have to mature in the ground, Alan is able to sow successionally from late spring until late summer. The high yield is ideal for the kitchen and saves them a substantial amount of money as they are an expensive crop to buy in from a supplier.

Alan's experimental crop red orach (*Atriplex hortensis*) also proved to be popular with the kitchen, providing the chefs with a highly flavoured, colourful and versatile ingredient that could be used raw or cooked. Akajiso – a purple form of perilla bought back by a friend from Japan – was another triumph for Alan. More commonly known as Japanese basil, it is a useful winter micro-crop or can be left to mature. It is ideal for tempura or stir-fries. Red-leaved shiso, another variety of perilla, tastes of aniseed, while the green variety has a cinnamon flavour. Amaranth however was not such a success, due largely to its bitter flavour when left uncooked. Though it could be wilted like spinach, with so much choice in wilted greens it needed to be more of an all-rounder crop. Whether good or bad, Alan relishes the chefs' feedback and finds it is essential to the success of the garden as well as making his job more satisfying.

The polytunnel at Monachyle Mhor provides invaluable protection in this part of Scotland. After trying the obvious crops – aubergines and tomatoes, which in the low light and colder temperatures produced a small yield but did not thrive, Alan is far more particular about what he grows in it now, preferring cut-and-come-again salads to replace heavily cropped plants and ensure a continuous supply of leaves, as well as introducing more exciting, unusual varieties.

Both Tom and Alan are keen to extend the growing space, and there are plans for another polytunnel, both to get vegetable crops off to an early start and to propagate herbaceous perennials to sell to guests. Alan also spotted the potential of using the ash from a new, wood-pellet burner system, which provides the hotel with a sustainable heating supply. He has mixed this ash with water, and in the growing season seaweed extract, to provide a feed for greedy plants that need plenty of resources to flower and fruit – like broad and runner beans, courgettes, cucumbers and squash.

BELOW Raised beds are invaluable for growing vegetables in the harsh climate of the Trossachs.

TWO-WAY RUNNER BEANS

SERVES 2

INGREDIENTS

Handful of runner beans
Butter, to dress the runner
    beans and to sauté the
    ceps and pancetta
2 ceps, trimmed and sliced
50g/2oz pancetta, thinly
    sliced
2 eggs
Toasted hazelnut oil

Runner beans have such a short season it is worth celebrating them any way you can. Just as the sweetness of peas heralds the start of summer, the earthy flavour of runner beans signals that autumn is nearly upon us.

METHOD

1   Cut half the runner beans into thin strips, then slice the remainder diagonally. Blanche all the beans in boiling water, remove, drain and finish with a knob of butter. Lightly sauté the ceps and pancetta in butter until golden brown. Meanwhile soft-poach the eggs.

2   Arrange the ceps, pancetta and runner beans on each plate, place the poached egg on top and drizzle with the toasted hazelnut oil.

ALAN & TOM'S
KITCHEN GARDEN SECRETS

- **Small gardens**: If space is limited, plan as accurately as possible what to grow and where to plant it out. It is sad to see crops sitting unhappily in pots, because you have no room for them, when they should be flourishing in the ground.
- **Start indoors**: To get an early start to the season begin germination indoors. This will also enable you to have more control when planting out, so the rows can be straight and plants set at the correct spacing.
- **Be patient**: When germinating seeds, try not to worry too much if seedlings do not appear as quickly as you would like. Persevere and keep the seed tray a little moist.
- **Cut frequently**: For cut-and-come-again salad leaves, Oriental greens and chard, harvest often to keep the crop young, tender and much tastier.
- **Plant care**: Harvest for the plant rather than for the plate. If a salad crop is getting too big, cut it back to encourage new fresh growth. Use the cut greens as you would spinach, rather than eating them raw.

RUNNER BEANS

One vegetable that did well in Alan's first season at Monachyle Mhor was runner bean 'Scarlet Emperor', even though it was only a small trial crop and was planted out in early summer. The plants produced a lot of flowers as well as bountiful harvests from late summer until early autumn. Alan recommends that runner beans have good fertile soil and, before planting, that you prepare a two-cane cross-structure or trellis for them to grow up. Such climbers reach up to 2.5m/8ft, but if space is an issue Alan suggests growing dwarf varieties as they are good early croppers, especially if you have a polytunnel or greenhouse. Warmth is needed to encourage bees to pollinate runner bean flowers.

LEAFY MUSTARD

One of the crops on which Alan uses horticultural fleece to protect against animals during the growing season is the mustard green 'Golden Frills' – a Chinese heritage variety that is a cross between kale and mustard. This large, lacy-leaved salad crop has a sweet and gently spicy flavour with a hint of potato. It is a vigorous variety that is hardy and suitable for cool weather.

MUSTARD CALENDAR

SOW Do this in early and mid-spring for harvesting between mid-spring and early summer, and sow again from early summer to early autumn for a late summer to late autumn crop. Start leafy mustard in a seed tray or direct sow.
HARVEST Cut with clean sharp scissors as a cut-and-come-again crop.

RUNNER BEAN CALENDAR

SOW In late spring sow under cover; do this in root-trainers as runner beans put down long roots, which should not be disturbed when they are planted out after the risk of frosts has passed. You can direct sow runner beans in early or midsummer once the soil has warmed up.
CARE Pinch out the growing tips when they reach the desired height. Water regularly, especially when the flowers appear, as this helps them to set and produce a crop.
HARVEST Pick regularly, to encourage more beans.

CITRUS-VANILLA-CURED VINEGAR TROUT

SERVES 2

INGREDIENTS

CURED FISH
Equal parts salt and caster sugar – enough to cover the fish
Juice of 2 lemons (or 4 oranges) and strips of their zests
Fresh vanilla pod, cut in half
2 filleted trout

SOURDOUGH CRISPS
2 tsp olive oil
Sprig of thyme
Rind of $^1/_2$ lemon
Salt and pepper to taste
2 thin slices of sourdough – it can be stale

VINAIGRETTE
200ml/$^1/_3$ pint orange juice
100ml/3$^1/_2$fl oz rapeseed oil
Salt and pepper
Burnt-orange 10-year-old Glengoyne whisky, to taste
$^1/_2$ lemon

TOASTED ALMOND DRESSING
100g/3$^1/_2$oz whole blanched almonds
20g/$^3/_4$oz unsalted butter
$^1/_2$ banana shallot
1 tsp finely chopped parsley
50ml/2fl oz olive pomace oil
50ml/2fl oz rapeseed oil
Salt and pepper

TO SERVE
Generous handful of mustard leaves

Instead of grinding pepper over cured fish, Tom uses mustard leaves to provide the same flavour and bring the dish alive. You want to taste the flavour of the whisky so there is no need to burn off the alcohol.

METHOD

1 **For the cured fish**, mix the salt, sugar, lemon (or orange) and vanilla pod together, then coat both sides of each trout fillet. Leave for 12 hours, or longer, depending on the thickness of the fillets.

2 **For the sourdough crisps**, combine the oil, thyme, lemon rind, salt and pepper. Grill the slices of sourdough and, just before they golden, remove from the heat and paint on the premixed ingredients. Return to the grill until golden.

3 **For the vinaigrette**, boil the orange juice in a saucepan until it is half its previous volume. Add the rapeseed oil, salt and pepper, then the whisky and a squeeze of lemon juice.

4 **For the toasted almond dressing**, heat up a frying pan on a medium heat and toss the almonds all the way round; finish with butter to toast them evenly. Finely chop the banana shallot and combine with the parsley, almonds and both oils. Season with salt and pepper, to taste.

5 **To serve**, arrange a trout fillet, mustard leaves and sourdough crisp on each plate. Lightly drizzle over the vinaigrette and toasted almond dressing.

13

VALLUM FARM

Northumberland

Specialist vegetable grower Ken Holland is causing quite a stir with the produce he is nurturing in the Tyne valley. He and his team, comprising his wife Tracy, brother-in-law Mark and apprentice Drew Tranter, look after about eighty varieties of vegetables, shoots and cresses on 3.2 hectares/8 acres of land on Vallum Farm: a 0.8-hectare/2-acre walled garden at Little Harle; a 0.8-hectare/2-acre kitchen garden; a 1.6-hectare/4-acre field; and six polytunnels.

In addition to traditional and heritage-variety baby vegetables and micro-crops (including the 600,000 baby carrots and 300,000 baby beetroot grown each year) Ken and his team also are groundbreaking with their experimental 'forcing' polytunnels, which protect crops of pea shoots, broad bean shoots, clamped beetroot leaves and nasturtium leaves. It is this sort of new approach to creating innovative and tasty crops that has resulted in a waiting list of customers, many of whom are Michelin-starred chefs, all wishing to use Ken's produce in their kitchens.

Ken is unconventional and likes to grow everything close together with the intention of getting some elongated crops alongside rounded produce. Radish works well sown and grown in this way, producing two rounded bulbs and one long one — the latter shape being chef Simon Rogan's preferred one for this crop. Although not officially certified as such, Ken and his team work organically, sowing, weeding and harvesting by hand.

TRADITIONAL VERSUS MODERN

The baby vegetables, for which Ken has an unrivalled reputation, particularly thrive in the microclimate of the walled garden. He prefers heritage varieties as they grow well in the soil, look good and are often more colourful and intensely flavoured than more modern varieties.

The range of produce is exciting and includes: 'Paris Market' and 'Kuttinger' carrots; 'Chioggia' and 'Albina Ice' beetroot; fifteen tomato varieties; courgettes; leeks; crosne or Chinese artichokes; lettuces; 'Crystal Lemon' cucumbers; as well as edible flowers including violets (*Viola odoratus*), nasturtiums (*Tropaeolum majus*) and pinks (*Dianthus*). The team at Vallum Farm decided to stop growing swede and cabbage in favour of superior, more high-valued crops, but are now considering whether or not to grow them in one of their other nearby fields.

Ken is passionate about the vegetables he grows, but he also takes more than a professional interest in how his produce is used in the kitchen. He works with a number of chefs to taste-test their vegetables and establish the best for flavour, texture and, of course,

The grower,
Ken Holland

The chef,
David Kennedy

OPPOSITE 'The Pod' at Vallum brings chef, grower and diners together to celebrate seasonality in an exciting innovative way.

appearance. In the kitchen garden at Vallum Farm is a chef's 'Pod' – a quirky wooden 'wagon' on wheels, kitted out with a kitchen and trestle 'chef's table' that seats twelve people. There are now quite literally only seconds between harvesting a crop from Ken's garden and a chef preparing it for a dish.

The resident chef at The Pod is the North-East's well-known David Kennedy ('DK'), who runs his own restaurant, David Kennedy at Vallum, 100 metres/110 yards from Ken's kitchen garden. Some guest chefs have also been invited to cook at the The Pod, including local icons Terry Laybourne and James Close from The Raby Hunt Restaurant. Plans are afoot for a night with Sat Baines, Tom Kerridge, Andrew Fairlie and Claude Bosi.

The close proximity of garden and kitchen as well as David's close working relationship with Ken have completely changed how he devises his recipes. David creates a collection of seasonal menus based around vegetables, with meat and fish a secondary element, and then tailors them each week to reflect

exactly what is ready to be harvested. First thing in the morning Ken may tell David that for example courgette flowers are ready for picking, and they then appear on the menu that lunchtime. This is the perfect grower/chef relationship from Ken's perspective – it frustrates him when a chef orders exact sizes and varieties for a specific day rather than appreciating it might be a few more days for some crops, or a week for another before they will be at their absolute best for gathering. Ken also enjoys discussing with David what to grow each season.

Apart from potatoes, which Ken is planning to start planting for David next season and one or two herbs, all the produce used in David's kitchen is from the kitchen garden, grown in beds Ken has set aside as 'DK' produce. Highlights for David have been the delicious apple marigold (*Tagetes minuta*) with a strong taste of green apple skin and a floral finish, which he likes to pair with crab and wood sorrel (*Oxalis*). He predominantly uses sorrel as a garnish but finds the tubers a much underrated crop. He parboils them and finishes them in a *beurre noisette* as an accompaniment with duck or other autumnal dishes.

BELOW LEFT Kale is a popular crop with chefs as it is available throughout the winter months.
BELOW RIGHT Kuri squash is a thick-skinned, winter variety from Japan.

WINTER SQUASH

Squash are great for the winter larder, and Ken grows a number of different varieties from butternut to the more unusual, round winter squash 'Uchiki Kuri', also known as Japanese squash, red kuri squash or onion squash. It is actually a heritage French variety and has a distinct chestnut flavour, which David suggests needs little enhancement before using it in recipes. He also recommends storing 'Uchiki Kuri' squash for at least a month after harvesting, to help the flavour develop further. If you do not have a lot of space for these easy-to-grow plants, you can plant squash in containers or train them up and over supports.

FLORENCE FENNEL

Both bulbs and flowers of Florence fennel are popular ingredients in the kitchen at David Kennedy at Vallum. To produce a long season of baby and micro-sized Florence fennel Ken grows them intensively in raised beds and sunny open ground as well as in a polytunnel over the winter. Before planting he works plenty of well-rotted organic matter into the free-draining soil. He keeps plants well watered to prevent bolting. Slugs love the juicy bulb and leaves, so Ken uses nematodes to keep them at bay or picks them off by hand.

WINTER SQUASH CALENDAR

SOWING PREPARATION Years of experience have resulted in Ken using weed-suppressing membrane over the squash bed to keep weeds at bay as well as to lock in moisture. A few weeks before planting he prepares planting holes by cutting through the membrane, to about a spade spit's depth and width, which he fills with well-rotted organic matter.

SOW Ken grows winter squash from seed, starting them off in the polytunnel in late winter and planting out seedlings in late spring.

CARE During the growing season Ken feeds winter squash every other week with organic chicken-manure pellets and seaweed liquid feed. They are also thirsty plants so he waters regularly too.

HARVEST He prefers to harvest the winter squash before they are too big. He removes any left on the plant before the risk of first frosts. When harvesting for storage Ken leaves some stalk on the squash and places it upside down, to help prevent rotting, in a cool dry room for up to three months.

FLORENCE FENNEL CALENDAR

SOW Fennel plants prefer not to be disturbed so Ken direct sows in the polytunnel from mid-spring and outdoors in raised beds from late spring, to ensure the longest season possible.

CARE Once established he feeds plants with high-potash fertilizer every few weeks. He also earths up the soil to cover the bulbs when they start to swell, thereby keeping them white and free from frost.

HARVEST David prefers the bulbs to be harvested when they are small, with the roots intact. The flowers are delicious too.

'UCHIKI KURI' SQUASH SOUP & A ROASTED WEDGE

SERVES 4

INGREDIENTS

1 medium-sized 'Uchiki Kuri' squash
20g/³/₄oz butter
Salt and pepper
2 sage leaves
400ml/²/₃ pint water
50ml/2fl oz rapeseed oil

Here David shows how to make soup from 'Uchiki Kuri' squash, without any other vegetables, so you get the full flavour of this variety of squash. Cheese scones are a good accompaniment.

METHOD

1 Peel and quarter the squash. Remove the seeds and put them and one-quarter of the squash aside for use later. Dice the remaining flesh. Melt the butter in a saucepan, then put in the diced squash and cook slowly, without it colouring, until soft. Season with salt and pepper, add the sage and water, and bring to the boil and simmer for 5 minutes. Liquidize and keep hot.

2 Cut the retained squash quarter into 4 even-sized wedges. Heat the oil in a frying pan and cook each squash wedge on all sides, then remove from the pan.

3 Throw in the retained squash seeds and cook until soft.

4 Serve the wedges alongside the soup, and sprinkle the seeds over the soup.

KEN & DAVID'S
KITCHEN GARDEN SECRETS

- **Quality veg**: Do not overwater baby vegetables so they can build a strong root structure.
- **Weed control**: Use weed-suppressing membrane as much as you can to cover your soil and thereby reduce the time you need to spend weeding.
- **Extending the season**: Keep sowing as late in the season as you can, providing the conditions for germination are still suitable.
- **Soil preparation**: Always use compost, preferably from your own heap, to topdress your growing areas at the start of every season.
- **Winter storage**: Clamp your root vegetables every year by storing them in a box or in a hole in the ground, building up layers of sand and individually laid-out root vegetables (do not let them touch). Use as you need them.
- **Try heritage varieties**: Ken believes if a type of vegetable has been grown for two hundred or so years it must be good. He is convinced that the flavours of most heritage varieties are superior to modern hybrids, bred to last and to combat disease.

NORTH SHIELD'S LANDED CRAB, FLORENCE FENNEL & TOASTED SOURDOUGH

SERVES 2

INGREDIENTS

100g/3^1/$_2$oz picked white crabmeat
50g/2oz brown crabmeat
Juice of ^{1}/$_2$ lemon
Salt and pepper

DRESSING
100ml/3^1/$_2$fl oz rapeseed oil
1 tbsp apple vinegar
1 tsp English mustard

FENNEL PESTO
Handful of fennel tops
2 tsp toasted pine nuts
2 tsp grated Parmesan cheese
100ml/3^1/$_2$fl oz rapeseed oil
^{1}/$_2$ garlic clove, grated
Salt and pepper

TOASTED SOURDOUGH
2 thin slices of sourdough
Rapeseed oil

TO SERVE
Handful of fennel tops
Spring onions, to garnish

David delights in the Florence fennel grown at Vallum Farm because of its flavour and the impact that it has for something so small. Also he uses all of this vegetable, from its root to its fronds, and likes to showcase its full potential.

METHOD

1 Combine both crabmeats with the lemon juice; then add salt and pepper, according to taste. Set aside.

2 **For the dressing**, whisk all the ingredients together. Set aside.

3 **For the fennel pesto**, combine all the ingredients in a liquidizer, and blend until smooth. Set aside.

4 **For the toasted sourdough**, preheat the oven to 180°C/350°F/ gas mark 4. Slice the sourdough as thinly as you can. Place the slices on a baking sheet, drizzle over some rapeseed oil, and bake for 5 minutes.

5 **To serve**, use 2 dessert spoons to mould some of the crabmeat, to form quenelles. Place 3 of these on each plate. Lightly coat the fennel tops with the dressing, and place around the crab. Dot around the fennel pesto, and finish with the toasted sourdough and spring onions.

14

THE SCOTTISH KITCHEN GARDEN

Midlothian

The initial idea behind chef Carina Contini's Scottish Kitchen Garden was to supply her two Edinburgh-based restaurants, The Scottish Café & Restaurant and Centotre, with a different fruit and vegetable variety each month. Among the many things she and her gardener, Erica Randall, have learnt on their journey since creating the garden from scratch in 2011 is that it is a question of what your garden will give to you rather than what you demand of it.

The Scottish Kitchen Garden is a 0.4-hectare/1-acre plot – part of Carina's own garden – in the beautiful Esk Valley Conservation Area lying just 8 kilometres/5 miles outside the capital city. Erica, who trained at the Royal Botanic Garden Edinburgh, was brought on board to oversee the restoration of the Victorian garden and transform it into a productive plot. Undeterred by a rather awkward 3m/10ft drop to one side and a boundary of tall trees, Erica, Carina and her husband and business partner, Victor, as well as a multitude of their family and friends completely cleared the ground, built twelve raised beds and erected a polytunnel.

Although it was hard work, Erica found that renovating the garden enabled her to get to know the plot better and work out the optimum positions for plants. She decided, for example, to grow Jerusalem artichokes under the sloping, tree-lined boundary as they do not mind a bit of shade, and being perennial would need to be planted only once, which was useful in this potentially troublesome spot. Raspberries, another perennial, would go in the main sloping bed, which would require only regular weeding and mulching rather than annual planting.

When it came to deciding which crops to grow and the best varieties, Erica and Carina turned to some of the restaurants' local suppliers, not only to continue supporting them but also more importantly to benefit from their knowledge about Scottish heritage varieties.

OPPOSITE Red orach (*Atriplex hortensis*) is an attractive plant that can be used as an alternative to spinach.
BELOW Erica's bothy, named after the patron saint of cooks, is a welcome retreat from the kitchen garden in cold and wet weather.

The grower,
Erica Randall

The chef,
Carina Contini

ERICA & CARINA'S
KITCHEN GARDEN SECRETS

- **Take care of the soil**: It is the most important resource a gardener has for growing healthy productive plants. Add plenty of organic matter and keep the soil covered with crops, green manures and mulches. Avoid damaging the structure of heavy soil by never working it or walking on it when wet.
- **Be vigilant**: Check plants daily to monitor changes in their growth and health. It is always easier to nip any problems early on to prevent them from spreading.
- **Watering**: Getting watering just right is often a skill in itself. By observing and paying attention to individual plants, their growing media and containers you can prevent all sorts of problems such as bolting, disease and scorch.
- **Try something new**: It is good to trial a new crop, cultivar or even technique each year. This allows you to find new flavours and ways to grow plants.
- **Gardening in harmony with nature**: Grow flowers, and even plants that you might consider to be weeds, to encourage beneficial insects and to increase the biodiversity of your garden. Most weeds have some benefits by, for example, making nutrient fertilizers, providing food for predatory insects or just giving you something else to eat.

Graham 'Mr Apple' Stoddart from Cuddybridge Apple Juice provided a number of different varieties, so Erica and Carina planted cordons of 'eaters' such as 'Peasgood's Nonsuch' on the south-facing wall as they develop better in sunlight, and 'cookers' such as the Edinburgh-bred 'James Grieve', 'Charles Ross' and 'White Melrose' on the west-facing wall. Perthshire-based Mr Pattullo of Glamis Asparagus supplied Erica and Carina with eighty crowns of French asparagus, choosing two varieties to extend the season, while David Craig of Clyde Valley Tomatoes recommended the heritage variety 'Ailsa Craig' because of its exceptional flavour. However growing tomatoes in The Scottish Kitchen Garden raises an interesting issue for Carina. While local provenance is important, so too is the taste of food, and with her Italian–Scottish dual heritage she finds the sunshine that ripens the tomatoes grown in Italy is extremely important and triggers a very different taste.

LEARNING PROCESS

Growing appropriate quantities for the restaurants was quite a challenge for Erica, and she freely admits that it is an issue resolved through trial and error. A bed of forced then maincrop rhubarb provides supplies for only a month, as does half a bed of broad beans. Salads are much easier to gauge, as Erica sows a range of varieties outdoors and in the polytunnel, and these provide the kitchen with almost year-round crops. In summer the netted salad bed is filled with mizuna, mibuna, pak choi and rocket and is then replaced with hardy winter lettuce, mustard leaves (under fleece), lamb's lettuce, chop-suey greens, coriander, chervil and spinach. She sows in wide drills and gets three decent cuts from one sowing.

Although peas grow well in The Scottish Kitchen Garden, harvesting the pods on a daily basis was extremely time-consuming and made the crop almost too costly for a single-gardener productive garden. Erica's solution was to grow peas for their tender shoots instead. She therefore sows the pea seeds thickly, which means that she can harvest generous quantities of shoots, almost as a cut-and-come-again crop.

Sometimes there is no easy answer to the time needed to harvest a crop – it can take two hours for

Erica to pick crops such as radish, leeks, courgettes and salad leaves, which provide just enough for twenty dishes on the menu. Such time-consuming tasks can be frustrating for Erica because it means other jobs have to wait. Carina however is convinced that it is time well spent, even though it makes The Scottish Kitchen Garden's produce an expensive alternative to those from local suppliers.

Carina's husband Victor delivers the morning harvest to the restaurants, while Erica likes to bring in the evening-service produce herself. She enjoys the opportunity to talk to the chefs and get their feedback on new varieties. She also gives a talk to the chefs a couple of times a year, about growing and seasonality. It is fun to get together and gives the whole team a chance to discuss what is and is not working. In such a session it was pointed out that nasturtium (*Tropaeolum majus*) flowers were popular but the chefs found the leaves to be too strongly flavoured, so they are now used to make pesto. Also the chefs liked baby carrot thinnings complete with

BELOW Nasturtiums are an easy crop to grow, and Carina's chefs use both the leaves and the flowers.

tops, to use in cocktails at Centotre. Beetroot too is a favourite with the chefs, who noticed the flavour was fresh, earthy and delicious. Such get-togethers are a great help to Erica when it comes to planning the garden each season.

RASPBERRIES

In order to provide the restaurants with raspberries for as long as possible each season, Erica grows summer varieties ('Malling Jewel', 'Glen Ample' and 'Tulameen') as well as autumn ones ('Autumn Bliss' and 'Fall Gold'). For these she chose the most sloping bed at The Scottish Kitchen Garden, as once planted they just need maintenance on this awkward site. Prior to planting, Erica cleared the area by soaking the soil and covering it with large sheets of cardboard, soaking these and then adding a generous layer of compost. While it slowly broke down, the cardboard acted as a weed suppressant and helped to lock in moisture. Fortunately the soil in The Scottish Kitchen Garden is slightly acidic and so provides the best growing conditions for the raspberries.

RASPBERRY CALENDAR

PLANT Put in bare-root canes (stems) in the dormant season. Erica set hers in rows and trained them along parallel lengths of wire, supported on posts, to provide summer varieties with plenty of air.
CARE Erica applies a feed in spring and ties in new growth along the wires during the growing season. After harvesting she cuts back the canes of summer-fruiting raspberries that have fruited to the ground and then ties in 6–8 vigorous new stems for each plant. For autumn-fruiting varieties, she cuts back all canes to ground level in late winter.
HARVEST She picks raspberries on a dry day, and when doing so knows how important it is to bend down and look upwards to spot hidden fruits.

RASPBERRY CRANACHAN

SERVES 6

Undoubtably, a Scottish classic. Although generally made with raspberries, for which Scotland is famous, cranachan can also be created with blackberries or tayberries, for a sharper contrast. Cranachan is really easy to do, provided you do not overbeat the cream. This simple summer party pudding can be made in advance and served with a few edible flowers or fresh mint from the garden, for that extra little sparkle.

INGREDIENTS

300g/10oz medium organic oatmeal
4 tbsp runny clover honey
100ml/3 ¹/₂fl oz very light lowland whisky or fruit liqueur
500ml/17 ¹/₂fl oz double cream
500g/1lb 1oz fresh raspberries
Mint leaves or edible flowers such as violas, to decorate

METHOD

1   Preheat the oven to 180°C/350°F/ gas mark 4. Combine the oatmeal and half the honey and then roast for about 10 minutes, until golden in colour. Keep a close eye on them as the oats can catch quickly and burn. Remove from the oven and, while hot, pour over the whisky or liqueur. The heat of the tray helps to evaporate the alcohol. Crumble the crisp oatmeal mixture and set aside. Whip the cream until soft but not stiff. Wash and dry the raspberries.

2   In a bowl, fold half the raspberries, the remaining honey and two-thirds of the toasted oatmeal and mix together. Fold this into the softly whipped cream. The mixture should be marbled with the raspberries and turn slightly pink.

3   **To serve**, spoon the creamy mixture into chilled glasses, scattering the remaining whole raspberries as you fill the glass. Decorate with the remaining toasted oats and a little mint or some edible flowers.

CHARD

This vegetable is a useful addition to a productive plot as it provides bountiful supplies of colourful stems and delicious leaves that can be harvested when they are small or be left to grow and used like spinach. Erica uses the top bed of the plot for chard as the site is relatively open there, though there is some shade in summer, which is fine for chard. The soil is well-draining and rich as Erica applies plenty of organic matter prior to planting out the seedlings. She plants more densely when chard is to be used as a cut-and-come-again crop, and keeps a watch out for downy mildew, which can cause seedlings to collapse if they are too close together. Birds can be a problem for direct-sown seedlings, but a net or mesh cover helps to protect the chard.

CHARD CALENDAR

SOW In spring start seeds off in 9cm/3½in pots under cover and thin out once the first true leaves appear. Successional sowing is also a good idea with chard if, like Carina, you prefer to use small leaves. You can direct sow chard from mid-spring if the soil is warm enough, and make a second sowing in midsummer for spring harvests. Erica makes her final sowings under cover in late summer.

HARVEST When harvesting, Erica removes the outer leaves first.

CARE Erica keeps chard well watered and if growing them outdoors uses a cloche to protect the plants. You could also cover them with straw or horticultural fleece to offer the same protection.

RAINBOW CHARD & BEAN SOUP

SERVES 4

Nothing satisfies more than a bowl of hearty warming soup when you need a bit of comfort. The fresh fennel gives a wonderful background flavour, while the fennel pesto provides an extra kick that you were really not expecting. This soup can easily be made without the sausage, but with Carina's Italian heritage she really cannot resist. For the perfect texture, blend (using a processor or a hand blender) about one-quarter of the soup to a smooth consistency and add this back into the chunky soup.

METHOD

1   Soak the beans overnight in a large pot with the bicarbonate of soda and lots of cold water. (The bicarbonate of soda helps release the nasty gases that cause some people to avoid beans because of their antisocial side effects.) The following day, rinse the beans and return to the pot with plenty of cold water. Bring the beans to the boil and then drain and rinse under a tap. In a large soup pot fry the onions, fennel and any non-tender stalks of the chard in the olive oil until soft and golden. The longer and slower this process takes, the better the flavours that will emerge later in the finished soup.

2   Add the stock and beans and bring to a simmer. Add salt and pepper, to taste. If you are using a ham stock you may not need to add any salt at this stage.

3   Remove the skin from the sausage and add to the soup pot in one piece. Simmer for 40–60 minutes, until the beans are soft. This will depend on how dry the beans were when you started and how long you soaked them for.

4   Roughly chop the chard leaves and finely chop the remaining tender stalks. Add these to the soup pot and simmer for about 5 minutes, until they have wilted. Check the seasoning.

5   **For the dried fennel pesto**, using a pestle and mortar cream the garlic with a pinch of salt. Add the parsley leaves and mix to a creamy consistency aided by the olive oil. Then add the fennel seeds and rosemary and gently work to a runny paste, adding more oil if required.

6   **To serve**, add a couple of spoonfuls of the dried fennel pesto to the soup. Serve piping hot.

INGREDIENTS

500g/1lb 1oz dried cannellini beans
1 tsp bicarbonate of soda
2 large onions, finely chopped
Large fennel bulb, finely chopped
500g/1lb 1oz rainbow chard
2 tbsp extra-virgin olive oil
1 litre/1¾ pints vegetable or ham stock
Salt and pepper
200g/7oz dried Italian Calabrese or Spanish chorizo sausage

DRIED FENNEL PESTO
2 garlic cloves, peeled
Salt
Large handful of parsley leaves, chopped
1 generous tbsp extra-virgin olive oil
2 tsp dried fennel seeds
2 tsp rosemary, very finely chopped

15

SIR TERENCE CONRAN & THE ALBION

Hampshire & London

It is amazing to think that ten years ago Sir Terence Conran, one of our best-known designers, restaurateurs and retailers, could have been found on his hands and knees in his beautiful walled potager at his Hampshire home. The fact that Sir Terence was picking 'Fraises des Bois' strawberries to take to one of his London restaurants is not in itself unexpected, but the combination of both Sir Terence and the then head chef at Bibendum, Simon Hopkinson, appreciating that this freshly picked, home-grown crop would be far superior to supplier-bought produce was ahead of the pack. At a time when most chefs were almost exclusively looking for exotic, expensive and experimental produce, wherever its origins, it is noteworthy that Sir Terence and some of his leading chefs were not. They were therefore among the forerunners of the professional kitchens', home-grown movement.

As he was one of the most celebrated restaurateurs it made good sense for Sir Terence to supply his restaurants – Bluebird, Le Pont de la Tour, Butlers Wharf Chop House, Bibendum, Coq d'Argent and the Blueprint Café – with home-grown produce from Barton Court. For Sir Terence, harvesting produce from his own kitchen garden was a question of using up the abundance of produce rather than generating a feel-good, public-relations story.

His head gardener at Barton Court, Jonathan Chidsey, had started work with Sir Terence in 1980, first as a trainee and then after six years as head gardener. The two of them collaborate about the best crops to grow as well as where to create new areas for produce to use in the restaurants. Two large

OPPOSITE The potager at Barton Court has provided produce for Sir Terence's restaurants for more than ten years.
BELOW An attractive gated wall separates the potager from the old orchard and herb beds.

The grower,
Jonathan Chidsey

The chef,
Sir Terence Conran

herb beds were dug out in the restored orchards just beyond the main potager, and in these Jonathan now grows twenty varieties of perennial herbs such as sage, tarragon, thyme and rosemary, which provide a harvest of 1,500 bunches each week, from late spring to early autumn. He cuts them back in late autumn and covers the more tender varieties such as some thyme and French tarragon with long cloches.

Nowadays, Sir Terence no longer has business interests in the restaurants and spends more time at his country house with family and friends, so the balance has shifted in favour of produce first finding its way to the kitchen at his country home and then to the professional kitchens. His most recent restaurant venture, The Albion at both Shoreditch and Tate Modern, are the beneficiaries, and Jonathan speaks to the chef or co-owner, Peter Prescott, at the start of each week to let him know what is ready in the

Barton Court kitchen garden – figs, apples, courgettes, tomatoes, chillis, edible flowers, salads and herbs are among the wide range of crops on offer.

Jonathan finds it funny that, in those early years, rocket was seen as exciting and exotic, organic seeds were hard to get hold of, and the extent of varieties was limited.

Sir Terence loves early summer vegetables – asparagus, early peas and broad beans and baby carrots (out of the greenhouse) – heralding the start of a bountiful season. He remains true to the idea that freshly picked, home-grown produce does not need much adornment and prefers to let the flavours speak for themselves.

Each season Jonathan makes a note of the varieties that perform well: for example, 'Gardener's Delight' tomatoes; 'Banana' and 'Queen of the North' bell peppers; 'Pink Fir Apple', 'Désirée' and 'Belle de Fontenay' potatoes; and Turk's Cap pumpkins. He also ensures that there is always something new to try. However, as the soil at Barton Court is free-

BELOW Jonathan planted the apple arches when he first joined the staff at Barton Court more than twenty-five years ago.

draining and gravelly, the growing conditions are difficult for parsnips, which are prone to forking.

Sir Terence's chefs always comment on the intense flavours of the produce from Barton Court, and Jonathan puts this down to a combination of the right variety and growing them in the excellent microclimate provided by a walled garden. As well as the flavour of the crops, the design of the walled garden is of importance. Though much of it had been laid out – in a traditional potager arrangement of rectangular beds edged in box hedging – before Jonathan joined the staff, he has added many clever features that are as much practical growing solutions as design follies. He softened the pathways in the walled garden, helping to create a gentle informal design, by planting wild strawberries at the edges and allowing them to creep into the pathways. They are easy to maintain too, and in mid- or late autumn he runs a lawnmower over them on a high setting to tidy them for the winter. Perhaps the most eye-catching feature that Jonathan has introduced at

Barton Court are the pumpkins that he grows on the large piles of leafmould beside the kitchen garden wall. Fuelled by such a convenient rich source of nutrients, the pumpkins grow vigorously and are trained up and over the wall so from both sides you see large orange or duck-egg-blue fruits defying gravity and hanging from their vines.

In winter Jonathan grows cavolo nero, broccoli, Brussels sprouts and leeks. As most winter vegetables need a year in the soil and are not that decorative, he scales down the range of what he grows during that season and concentrates on general upkeep and planning for the following year. Digging locally sourced manure into all the beds, by hand, takes about two months. Looking at Sir Terence's kitchen garden, such hard work is clearly the way to ensure a bountiful crop of year-round fruit and vegetables.

BELOW LEFT One of Sir Terence's favourite crops are tomatoes, which he likes to use in a simple salad.
BELOW RIGHT Jonathan cleverly maximizes space in the potager by allowing pumpkins and squash to climb up and over a wall.

AUBERGINES

At Barton Court Jonathan sows 'Black Beauty' or 'Bonica' varieties of aubergine. They need intense heat so he positions them anywhere that is south-facing, such as against a south-facing wall, which reflects heat. He also uses small pots, to restrict root space. He feeds plants once a week with a tomato feed, which he uses for all his crops. In warm weather he put the pots outdoors in early summer, and by early autumn the plants are producing good-sized fruit. If you prefer to grow aubergines in a greenhouse, Jonathan suggests combating whitefly and red spider mite with natural predators, as he prefers not to spray edible crops. Grafted plants can be a good alternative as they are more vigorous and can cope with cooler climates.

LEEKS

Jonathan uses two different techniques depending on when the crop is required. For winter leeks such as 'Blue Solaise' he makes individual holes with a dibber and drops a young leek plant into each one, waters well and leaves the plants to produce big crops, improved by frosts. Meanwhile he keeps the stems white by drawing up the soil as they grow. He waters regularly, and keeps the area well weeded. If it is a long wet season and leeks are planted closely together, they are likely to succumb to fungal leek rust, so he disposes of infected leaves at once.

For summer-cropping leeks, Jonathan recommends 'King Richard' or 'Nipper' varieties for intense flavour; also they need hardly any cooking. He sows them, leaves them to grow in a clump and never thins.

RATATOUILLE

SERVES 4

A classic summer vegetable stew that has many variations. Should the vegetables be cooked separately and be mixed together only at the final stage? Should you use red or green peppers? Do you cook ratatouille on the top of the stove or in the oven? Well this is Sir Terence's recipe, which he has developed through experimentation. This ratatouille is best left for 24 hours before eating, to give it a nice firm texture.

INGREDIENTS

200ml/¹/₃ pint olive oil
6 courgettes, sliced
3 onions, sliced
2 red peppers, cored, deseeded and sliced
2 aubergines, quartered and thickly sliced
4 garlic cloves, finely sliced
8 tomatoes, skinned, deseeded and quartered
Salt and pepper
Large sprig of thyme
Bay leaf

METHOD

1   Preheat the oven to 180°C/350°F/gas mark 4. Heat half the oil in a large frying pan and sauté the courgettes gently. When softened and turning golden, transfer them to an ovenproof casserole, leaving as much oil as possible in the frying pan.

2   Cook the onions gently in the frying pan, until wilted; then add to the courgettes in the casserole. Sauté the red peppers in the frying pan until softened, and add them to the casserole. Add more oil to the frying pan if required and cook the aubergines until they are just turning golden. Transfer them to the casserole.

3   Gently sauté the garlic until it just turns transparent, then add the tomatoes to the frying pan. Season with salt and pepper and cook until the tomatoes have become very soft. Together with the thyme and bay leaf, tip the garlic and tomatoes into the casserole, stirring gently to distribute the tomatoes among the other vegetables.

4   Cover with a lid and cook in the oven for 20 minutes. Take off the lid and cook for a further 35 minutes.

5   Add the remaining olive oil and allow to cool completely. Then cover the casserole again and keep the contents for 24 hours before serving at room temperature.

JONATHAN & SIR TERENCE'S
KITCHEN GARDEN SECRETS

- **Vertical courgettes**: If you are short of space in your garden sow climbing courgettes. The variety 'Black Forest' is a strong grower and will reach 1.75m/6ft tall. Vertically grown courgettes are much easier to pick than those on bushy plants, so you will not end up overlooking some of the fruits.
- **Leafmould**: If you have a large pile of autumn leaves try planting pumpkins on them. The heat generated by the rotting process will encourage the growth of very large pumpkins and will cover an unsightly corner of the plot.
- **Double duty**: A good example of companion planting is placing nasturtiums (*Tropaeolum majus*) next to your brassicas. Not only does this look colourful but the nasturtiums also attract cabbage white butterflies, and hopefully they will lay their eggs on the flowers and not on your precious cabbages.
- **Confine roots**: Grow chillies, sweet peppers and aubergines in 25cm/10in pots rather than in open ground, as a restricted root space will encourage plants to produce a heavier and healthier crop.
- **Baby leeks**: These make a nice summer substitute to spring onions. Sow as normal but do not thin out.

LEEKS VINAIGRETTE

SERVES 4

INGREDIENTS

8 slender leeks, trimmed and cleaned
2 hard-boiled eggs, coarsely chopped or put through a
   potato ricer, to garnish

VINAIGRETTE
2 tbsp red wine vinegar
14 tsp olive oil
2 tbsp Dijon mustard
Salt and pepper

When they are young and slender, leeks make an ideal light starter or vegetable accompaniment. Very thin leeks can be hard to come by, so if you cannot source them use larger ones, split lengthways – this dish will still work well. The intense flavour of the vinaigrette (yes, two tablespoons of Dijon mustard!) really lifts the whole dish perfectly.

METHOD

1 Put the leeks into a large shallow saucepan of slightly salted, boiling water; cook for 7–10 minutes. Remove the cooked leeks and drain thoroughly.

2 **For the vinaigrette**, mix the vinegar, olive oil and mustard together. Season with salt and pepper.

3 **To serve**, arrange the leeks on a shallow dish and drizzle them with lots of vinaigrette. Strew the chopped eggs over the leeks and pour the rest of the vinaigrette over the finished dish.

16

THE WELLINGTON ARMS

Hampshire

Simon Page and chef Jason King are hands-on when it comes to growing vegetables and fruit for their pub, The Wellington Arms, in Hampshire. Both enjoyed gardening before buying the pub in 2005, and were not fazed by the overgrown garden that came with the property. They have a helpful team supporting them too – anyone from their team in the pub or kitchen who has an interest in the garden has pitched in over the years.

The garden had humble beginnings, starting with two large troughs, which were filled with ornamental shrubs and positioned in front of the pub, primarily to deter customers from parking too closely. In the next couple of years after Simon and Jason bought The Wellington Arms, and when funds and time allowed, they cleared the garden and planted a herbaceous border, laid out four raised beds, established a mini-orchard and put up a polytunnel. The raised beds are made from sturdy sleepers. They are beautifully designed, with a box ball at each of the four corners and strawberry plants providing the remainder of the 'edging'.

Growing their own vegetables determines what features on the menu. One of Jason's popular dishes is twice-baked soufflé, and depending on the season it is adapted to incorporate asparagus, followed by leek and courgette and then spinach.

Courgette and pumpkin flowers are a menu highlight too, and are a prized crop, as they are expensive and difficult for a wholesaler to supply. They grow in abundance at The Wellington Arms, because Simon and Jason have taken the unorthodox step of

OPPOSITE Topiary box balls are used to add an element of design and structure to the raised beds.
BELOW Containers filled with herbs and herbaceous plants help Simon and Jason make the most of their growing space.

The grower,
Simon Page

The chef,
Jason King

growing them in a 'hot' polytunnel. Recognizing that the UK summers are unpredictable, they keep the doors shut to create a humid environment and plant their courgettes and pumpkins on a bed of horse manure, which rots down in the heat, creating a 'hot bed'. They also feed the plants regularly with appropriate nutrients. The approach has worked well, and during the growing season they harvest twenty flowers a day from six plants. Simon and Jason have made good use of limited space too by planting tomatoes in the same bed as the courgettes, and simply removing the first few leaves of the tomato plants, up to about 30cm/12in, so they do not block out light from the courgettes and pumpkins.

Plums are a highlight as well, being used for savoury and sweet dishes. In their small orchard are several trees that Jason thinks are a cross between a plum and a damson – the fruit is large yet with the tart flavour of a damson. He is keen to capture their

BELOW LEFT Simon propagates the strawberries and uses them to edge the raised beds as well as in oak barrels.
BELOW RIGHT A great tip from Simon and Jason is to cover unattractive pots in hessian cloth.

flavour and colour to use in dishes year-round, and so he stews the bulk of the crop and then freezes it.

Simon and Jason have not bought salads for years as they grow mizuna, red and green oak leaf lettuce, mustard 'Golden Streaks' and giant mustard chard. One of the reasons for the success of these crops in the garden and kitchen is that pests such as slugs do not seem keen on their peppery leaves.

VARIED PRODUCE

While Simon and Jason raise some crops from seed, they also work with a family-owned garden nursery, White Tower, in nearby Aldermaston, as it provides many weird and wonderful varieties. The staff at White Tower are also an invaluable source of advice, suggesting for example that Simon and Jason grow crops successionally to extend the seasons or try different varieties such as 'Purple Haze' carrots or 'Black Krim' heritage tomatoes.

They also grow herbs in oak barrels, square zinc tubs and containers wrapped stylishly in hessian by their housekeeper, Rosie. These individual pots of rosemary, thyme, tarragon, mint and parsley,

which Simon has artistically placed outside the back door, jostle together – a mix of vibrant greens and interesting textures. They look gorgeous, and for Jason and Simon they are also the best way to obtain the freshest leaves. Meanwhile fennel, chives, marjoram and borage are planted in borders alongside sweet peas (growing up tepees for height) and roses (for splashes of colour). Combining ornamental varieties alongside edible ones is a tip Simon and Jason picked up from a trip to the famous Château de Villandry, in France. It is a clever trick to use if space is an issue and you want your borders to look good for as long as possible.

Being avid recyclers Simon and Jason have eight biological digesters hidden around the garden, which is an efficient way to use up the kitchen waste. The chickens, sheep and a pig at The Wellington Arms provide a supply of manure to add to the compost. They have a four-bay system in which the compost is turned twice a month, ready to dig into the beds and borders in autumn. The raised beds and borders are covered with this traditional home-made compost, as well as a thick layer of a bio-compost, which Simon and Jason buy in a 10-tonne load each year from their local council. The bio-compost is great for suppressing weeds and protecting perennials from the cold, and it removes the need to weed or dig, as it breaks down naturally over the winter. Importantly for Simon and Jason too, the bio-compost creates a blanket of neat black soil that looks stylish and sets off plants such as heucheras and hostas. One thing is for certain at The Wellington Arms: in addition to the produce being plentiful and delicious, the garden always looks fantastic too.

SHALLOTS

Simon and Jason sow banana shallots so that the plants can put on shoots over the winter and are ready to grow vigorously by spring. At the same time in the remaining three beds they plant garlic and red onions. They love the uniform rows of green spikes, poking out above the soil during the cold months – appearance is important to both Simon and Jason. They then leave these low-maintenance crops until late spring or early summer, depending on the season, when they lift the small bulbs and wet garlic to allow room for runner beans. Simon and Jason find these alliums need little encouragement, and once harvested they are dried and plaited by the talented Rosie, and hung around the fireplace inside the pub. As the shallots do not keep very well, Jason soaks them in salt for a week and then pickles them. The garlic stores well, and the red onions are put in the refrigerator and used within a few weeks while they are in optimum condition.

SHALLOT CALENDAR

PLANT In late autumn Simon and Jason plant shallots as sets, sourced from their local nursery, rather than sowing seeds. The sets establish more quickly than seeds and provide better resistance against slugs. They plant them 25cm/10in apart in rows 40cm/16in apart, and water them well.
HARVEST The shallots should be ready for harvesting by late spring or early summer.

SIMON & JASON'S
KITCHEN GARDEN SECRETS

- **Be clever with space**: Jason and Simon underplant tomatoes with courgettes and pumpkins to get double the crop from the same space. This is essential when you have limited room in which to grow plants.
- **Biological digester**: Use the 'Green Cone' composter to transform food waste into a liquid feed that seeps into the ground. Available from some councils or online.
- **Long season**: Extend the seasons by successively planting crops where possible or by researching the best varieties to provide early, main and late crops.
- **Sprouting seeds**: In Jason's opinion sprouting seeds are much better than micro-crops, being more textured and flavourful, and are very easy to grow in a glass jar on a windowsill. Companies now specialize in providing organic fresh seed that is easy to grow.
- **Mini-potager**: Create a mini-potager in a bed or border. Ornamental plants provide colour and texture often when your vegetables are either small and uninteresting or else when they are going over and looking untidy.

GAME TERRINE OF VENISON, RABBIT, WOOD PIGEON & PORK WITH OUR BRAMLEY APPLE CHUTNEY & PICKLED SHALLOTS

SERVES 10

INGREDIENTS

TERRINE
200g/7oz minced venison from the shoulder or leg
1 boneless wild rabbit, with its heart, kidney and liver
2 boneless wood pigeon, with their hearts and livers
300g/10oz free-range belly pork
150g/5oz free-range pork fat or speck
Salt for the confit, plus 1 tsp salt
1 tbsp duck fat
3 juniper berries, crushed
2 sprigs of thyme, with the stems removed
1 tsp mace
2 cloves garlic, finely chopped
1 1/2 tsp pepper
20 thin slices of pancetta
4 bay leaves

BRAMLEY APPLE CHUTNEY
1.5kg/3 1/3lb cooking apples, peeled and diced
350g/12oz onions, finely chopped
200g/7oz muscovado soft dark brown sugar
400ml/2/3 pint malt vinegar
1 tbsp chilli powder or flakes
200g/7oz raisins
2 pieces, 7cm/3in long, of fresh root ginger, grated
1 tbsp fennel seeds
4 cloves
1 tsp ground coriander seeds

SHALLOT BRINE
1 litre/1 3/4 pints water
250g/9oz coarse rock salt
500g/1lb 1oz small banana shallots, peeled but leaving the root
    cores intact

PICKLING LIQUID
10 whole black peppercorns
5 fennel seeds
2 cloves
2 bay leaves
10 coriander seeds
1 litre/1 3/4 pints malt vinegar
180g/6oz brown sugar
2 red Dutch chillies, sliced thickly on the diagonal
2.5cm/1in piece of fresh root ginger, crushed

TO SERVE
Extra-virgin olive oil, to dribble
Pepper

You may be lucky enough to have a cousin in the family with a gun, to provide you with the odd bit of game. However, if you do not, Jason suggests you ask your butcher in advance to bone and coarsely mince the game for you. At The Wellington Arms Jason confits the livers and hearts and put them into the terrine whole, to create an interesting cross section when the terrine is sliced and served. Alternatively you could mince them into the mix. Your terrine will taste better over time, so remember to make it a few days in advance. A really good tip from Jason is to retain the pickling liquid from the shallots as it can be used again for many things, such as a base for chutney, escabeche or even more pickles. You simply have to strain your liquid and reboil it before using a second time.

METHOD

1 **For the terrine,** on the largest setting of your mincer, pass through the venison, rabbit, wood pigeon, pork belly and pork fat (or speck). To confit the livers, hearts and kidneys cover them with salt and leave overnight.

2 The following morning, preheat the oven to 160°C/325°F/gas mark 3. Wash the salt off the offal. Warm a little duck fat in a saucepan and add the offal; cover with tinfoil, then cook in the oven, until tender. Mix together with crushed juniper berries, thyme leaves, mace, garlic, 1 tsp salt and pepper. Cover with clingfilm and allow to infuse overnight in the refrigerator.

3   The following morning, preheat the oven to 160°C/325°F/gas mark 3. Line a terrine mould with tinfoil, triple-folded for strength, with extra overhanging 'handles', to allow you to remove the terrine in one piece when cold. Layer some of the pancetta into the terrine mould, overlapping each piece and overhanging some of them at the top of the mould. Press the minced game firmly into the mould, to ensure a smooth shape. Randomly add the confit offal. Top with the bay leaves and then the remaining pancetta. Cover the top of terrine with tinfoil. Bake in the oven for about 2 hours in a bain-marie (water bath). To test if it is cooked, insert a metal skewer into the centre of the terrine. It should come out hot if the terrine is cooked. When cooked, remove the terrine from the oven and leave to cool slightly. About an hour later place a heavy object on top of the terrine to press it down, until it is needed. (Jason uses an old house brick covered in tinfoil and clingfilm.)

4   **For the bramley apple chutney**, combine all ingredients in a large, heavy-based saucepan with a lid. Simmer on a moderate heat for an hour, stirring often. Remove the lid and continue cooking for another hour, or until you have a smooth paste. Store in the refrigerator in an airtight container or glass jar. This chutney keeps for several months.

5   **For the shallot brine**, bring the water to the boil in a large, stainless-steel saucepan and then add the salt so it dissolves. Leave to cool. When cold, add the shallots and let the brine stand for 5 days in the refrigerator. Then remove the shallots from the brine and rinse them well.

6   **For the pickling liquid**, place the peppercorns, fennel seeds, cloves, bay leaves and coriander seeds in a spice bag (a muslin square tied up with string). Bring the malt vinegar and sugar to the boil, add the spice bag, chillies and root ginger and leave to cool.

7   **For the pickled shallots**, place the brined shallots in a large sterilized glass pickling jar with a lid and pour over the pickling liquid. Seal with the lid, and store in the refrigerator for at least 2 weeks before use. The shallots will benefit from being in the pickling liquid for as long as possible, and will keep for almost 6 months in a refrigerator.

8   **To serve**, remove the terrine from the mould using the tinfoil handles, and carefully peel off the tinfoil. Cut into thick slices (1–2cm/½–¾in each). Drizzle a little olive oil on to the surface of the terrine (to enhance its colour and make it shiny) and then garnish with pepper. Serve with the bramley apple chutney, pickled shallots, a mixed salad and chargrilled hot toast.

STRAWBERRY CALENDAR

PLANT Strawberries like sun but need shelter too, so insects can easily reach the flowers. Choose fertile, well-drained soil and plant in autumn. If propagating from runners, plant them in autumn. Plant out in prepared holes, which should be big enough for the strawberry roots. To prevent rotting or the plants drying out, allow the bases of the crowns to rest on the soil surface. Backfill the planting holes and water well.

HARVEST Harvest perpetual strawberries from early summer to mid-autumn.

STRAWBERRIES

For The Wellington Arms, perpetual strawberries are a ubiquitous crop that is both ornamental as well as delicious when used in ice cream or a cordial. These strawberries have smaller yields and smaller fruits than summer-fruiting ones, but are ideal for a longer cropping season. Simon and Jason initially grew a few plants in hanging baskets, and they propagated their runners successfully at the end of each growing season so now they have a plentiful supply of these plants. Although typically grown in rows in a bed, Simon and Jason use their strawberry plants to edge each of the four raised beds, maximizing the space they have for other crops as well as creating an attractive feature. Raised beds also encourage deep roots. Usefully, perpetual strawberries are low-maintenance too; they are cut back just once after the first frosts, ready to reappear the following spring.

ABOVE and BELOW To propagate strawberries, remove a runner from a parent plant (1). Shorten the length of the runner, leaving the plantlet (2). Fill a 23cm/9in pot with potting compost, water and plant the strawberry plantlet (3). Firm the compost around the roots (4). Keep the compost well watered, and plant out when the roots of the young strawberry are established.

ELDERFLOWER CORDIAL & STRAWBERRY PUNCH

SERVES 10

During spring Jason makes many bottles of cordial to use in the bar at The Wellington Arms throughout the year. For this, he picks the elderflowers in the morning, before the bees get to them. He recommends including tartaric acid, as the cordial will then last much longer. Without the acid, the cordial will ferment within a month. You can buy it from a chemist.

METHOD

1 **For the elderflower cordial**, pick over the elderflowers removing any bugs, leaves or brown bits. Put the flowers into a large bowl, and cover with the boiling water, then add the lemon rind and orange rind. Cover and leave overnight in a cool place. Strain the liquid through a fine sieve; squeeze the pulp to extract all the juice.

2 Measure the amount of strained flower liquid. To every 550ml/1 pint strained flower liquid add 375g/13oz sugar, 4 tbsp lemon juice and (if you are using it) 1 tsp tartaric acid. Warm the strained flower liquid in a saucepan, to dissolve the sugar. Bring to the boil and skim off any scum. Allow the cordial to cool, and then strain through muslin or a brand-new, multipurpose, perforated cleaning cloth. Store the cordial in screw-top or corked bottles. You could even freeze it in batches in plastic containers.

3 **For the strawberry purée**, wash and hull the strawberries. Place them in a blender and purée with the sugar. Pass through a fine strainer and reserve until needed.

4 **To serve**, mix equal parts strawberry purée and elderflower cordial in a large jug, then fill the jug with crushed ice, borage flowers, lemon wedges and sprigs of mint. Dilute the elderflower and strawberry punch with a similar quantity of soda or sparkling water. Pour into tall glasses, each with some of the crushed ice, a wedge of lemon, a sprig of mint and a borage flower.

INGREDIENTS

ELDERFLOWER CORDIAL
40 heads of elderflower
1 litre/1³/₄ pints boiling water
Rind and juice of 3 lemons
Rind of 2 oranges
1.4kg/3lb granulated sugar
Tartaric acid (optional)

STRAWBERRY PURÉE
1kg/2lb 3oz strawberries
100g/3¹/₂oz caster sugar

TO SERVE
Crushed ice
10 borage flowers, to decorate
10 wedges of lemon
10 sprigs of mint
Soda or sparkling water

WINTERINGHAM FIELDS

17

Lincolnshire

Colin McGurran and his family took over Winteringham Fields, which is in a village near Scunthorpe, in 2005. He was known in the catering profession as having a genuine passion for provenance, and so grasped the opportunity in 2007 to take control of his vegetable supplier's 3.25 hectares/8 acres of land, which was for sale because of the supplier's ill-health. Under the watchful eye of his supplier and faced with a steep learning curve about soil type, forking carrots and frost pockets, Colin together with his right-hand man, sous-chef Slawek Mikolajczyk, and his team of eight chefs now grow produce for the restaurant at Winteringham Fields.

The farmland is a stone's throw from the restaurant and is divided into two fields. One field has light soil and so is suitable for root vegetables such as beetroot, onions, carrots and parsnips. The other one has good loam over clay soil, so is good for cabbages. Colin also has raised beds in the garden at Winteringham Fields, as well as a polytunnel to start off seedlings and extend the seasons.

He believes a kitchen garden is important because it helps chefs to understand the growing process and by growing it yourself you can recognize what is ripe and ready to be harvested. He also finds it fun to educate young chefs who see, often for the first time, how crops such as Brussels sprouts are grown, harvested and then served.

Unusually for a professional kitchen the entire team at Winteringham Fields takes an active role in growing the produce and collectively plans the growing season ahead, based on how crops fared the previous year. The staff also consider planting times according to each variety and work out what is viable, in terms of flavour and interest as an ingredient as well as financial return. They follow a traditional, four-year rotation system and spend at least an hour a day out in the fields or in the raised-bed gardens. Growing organically, though not certified, means it is difficult to defend crops against pests – the rabbits and hares in particular. For Colin and his team, this is local produce at its best and so, in season, these animals will appear on the menu too.

The team have had failures, though these have proved to be helpful rather than demoralizing. In the early years the polytunnel proved to be a challenge: for example, one season's crop of tomatoes suffered from overheating and then insufficient water. An irrigation system resolved this issue, but the following year they fed the crops too much and so too much leafy growth appeared. Colin is keen that his staff learn from any mistakes and continue to try out new and exciting ideas.

The chef/grower,
Colin McGurran

The sous-chef/grower,
Slawek Mikolajczyk

OPPOSITE Colin and Slawek have grown vegetables at Winteringham Fields for the last six years.

Given the extensive growing area, Colin and his team are able to raise enough produce to supply the kitchen's forty covers a day. They plant staples such as onions, garlic and potatoes, which smaller kitchen gardens might have to sacrifice in favour of a higher-value crop, and they are fortunate enough to be able to grow surplus crops to feed the pigs – they cultivated 10,000 carrots in one season.

The polytunnel and raised beds are set aside for more unusual varieties or crops that need a little more attention, such as courgettes, strawberries, tomatoes, salad leaves, herbs and edible flowers. Nothing is wasted, and the small tender baby roots and fruits appear on the menu while the bigger, more mature crops are used to feed their thirty-five staff at lunchtime.

During the bountiful seasons the kitchen at Winteringham Fields has to source only olive oil, nuts and citrus fruits from outside suppliers. For these, as well as when buying other essential ingredients if a crop has failed or there is not enough meat, Colin insists his staff go first to local suppliers. If venturing farther afield they use specialist suppliers with the same approach towards the best-quality, seasonal produce as they have at Winteringham Fields.

CABBAGE CALENDAR

SOW Colin sows summer varieties in polytunnels from late winter and transplants them in late spring, while mid-spring-sown winter cabbages are planted out in early summer and spring cabbages are sown in midsummer and transplanted in early autumn.
CARE Colin and his staff water the plants well when heads start to form, and feed the plants too.
HARVEST They crop the cabbages year-round.

CABBAGE

Colin and Slawek use this versatile ingredient raw, roasted, boiled and pickled, so they grow red, white and purple varieties as well as savoury and summer-hearting ones. They prepare the ground in the field well in advance, applying a layer of their farmyard manure in autumn. Only a day or so before sowing they use a tractor to plough the earth, rake it, compress it and rake it smooth and firm again. When harvesting the cabbages, they have experimented with leaving the stems in the ground to sprout again. They have also gathered just the small hearts of the open cabbages so that the kitchen can have a small tender ingredient as well as baby leaves a few weeks later.

COLIN & SLAWEK'S
KITCHEN GARDEN SECRETS

- **Retain flavour**: Store potatoes, onions and tomatoes in a cool dry place, not the refrigerator as the cold ruins the flavour.
- **Optimum condition**: Leaving the dirt on root veg like carrots, parsnips and beetroot helps them to last longer.
- **Companion planting**: Leeks repel carrot fly, and carrots repel onion fly and leek moth.
- **Faster gemination**: Soak parsnip and parsley seeds for hours, or even overnight, in room-temperature water.
- **Cabbage sprouts**: When harvesting the mature head of a cabbage, cut the stem 7–10cm/ 3–4in above ground level. You can then gather a later crop of cabbage sprouts, which develop on the stump.
- **Brassica flowers**: Leave kale in the ground over winter, and the following spring you can enjoy amazingly tasty flowers. You can do the same with all vegetables from the cabbage family.
- **Onion crops**: When onion tops begin to dry out and fall over, push the rest of the tops over too. Wait a week and dig up the bulbs. Spread the bulbs out in the sun for one week, to toughen the skins. Store in a dark place.

WINTERINGHAM WOOD PIGEON WITH HOME-GROWN CABBAGE & SPRING ONION

SERVES 4

INGREDIENTS

ONION OIL
5 large banana shallots, finely sliced
500ml/17½fl oz vegetable oil

CONFIT PIGEON LEGS
8 pigeon legs
Coarse sea salt
Sprig of thyme
Garlic clove
Sprig of rosemary

BARBECUE BABY SAVOY
CABBAGE
4 baby Savoy cabbages
Salt and pepper

OFFSHOOT RED CABBAGE
12 offshoot red cabbages
50g/2oz unsalted butter
Star anise
Salt and pepper

PICKLED CABBAGE
100g/3½oz caster sugar
100ml/3½fl oz white wine vinegar
Sprig of thyme
Sprig of rosemary
Bay leaf
Young red cabbage leaves
Sweetheart cabbage leaves

SPRING ONION SIDE DISH
50ml/2fl oz olive oil
4 spring onions, sliced lengthways
20g/¾oz butter
Salt and pepper

TO SERVE
1 whole wood pigeon
2 tsp onion oil
Sprig of thyme
Salt and pepper
Nasturtium leaves, to garnish
Marigold (*Tagetes*) flowers and
    leaves, to garnish

There is a plentiful source of wood pigeons in the vicinity of Winteringham Fields. These plump birds are used to create this dish with ingredients from within 8 kilometres/5 miles of the restaurant itself, which makes us very proud.

METHOD

1   **For the onion oil**, dry the sliced shallots on a cloth. Heat the oil to 140°C/275°F. Fry the shallots for 2 minutes until golden brown. Drain, and reserve the oil.

2   **For the confit pigeon legs**, cover the legs with the salt for 2 hours. Wash thoroughly and then cook them, together with the thyme, garlic and rosemary, for 2 hours in a 70°C/158°F bain-marie (water bath). Remove the thigh bone from each leg and trim.

3   **For the barbecue baby Savoy cabbage**, preheat a ceramic-shelled, lidded barbecue to 200°C/400°F/gas mark 6. Trim the cabbages by removing the larger leaves. Halve each one and season with salt and pepper. Cook for 4 minutes in the lidded barbecue.

4   **For the offshoot red cabbage**, peel the leaves of the cabbages until each is about the size of a quail's egg. Melt the butter in a small saucepan and add the star anise. Season the cabbage with salt and pepper, add it to the saucepan and cook for 2 minutes, until tender.

5   **For the pickled cabbage**, bring the sugar, vinegar, thyme, rosemary and bay leaf to the boil. Using a small cutter, cut round discs from the red cabbage and sweetheart cabbage leaves and pickle them for 5 minutes, before serving.

6   **For the spring onion side dish**, add olive oil to a hot saucepan and caramelize the spring onions for about 2 minutes, until golden brown. Add the butter and season with salt and pepper, to taste.

7   **To serve**, prepare the pigeon and remove the two breasts. Vacuum-pack the breasts with the onion oil, thyme, salt and pepper. Seal and cook in a bain-marie (water bath) for 15 minutes at 68°C/154°F. Meanwhile caramelize the confit pigeon legs skin-side down. When the pigeon breasts are cooked, garnish with nasturtium leaves and marigold flowers and leaves. Serve immediately, together with the confit pigeon legs, barbecued cabbage, offshoot cabbage, pickled cabbage and spring onion side dish.

WINTERINGHAM FIELDS POLYTUNNEL SALAD

SERVES 10

INGREDIENTS

BARBECUE BABY CARROTS
4 baby carrots

PICKLED BABY CARROTS
100g/3^1/$_2$oz caster sugar
100ml/3^1/$_2$fl oz white wine vinegar
Sprig of thyme
Sprig of rosemary
Bay leaf
4 baby carrots

BABY BEETROOT
8 red and golden baby beetroot
50g/2oz butter
Salt and pepper

BASIL PURÉE
300g/10oz courgettes
30g/1oz basil
30g/1oz butter
30ml/1fl oz double cream
Pinch of salt

CONFIT CHERRY TOMATOES
4 cherry tomatoes
Garlic clove, sliced
Sprig of thyme
Salt and pepper
1 tsp icing sugar
Olive oil, to drizzle
Lemon juice, to drizzle

ONION CROUTONS
2 slices of onion bread (heavy),
    frozen
2 tbsp onion oil

TO GARNISH
Baby rocket
Borage flowers
Pea shoots
Purple pea pods
Cucumber flowers
Redcurrants
Mustard leaves
Fennel

This very fresh, seasonal salad is picked just a few hours before it is served on the plate. As the ingredients are all fresh they still have a delicious earthy taste, which a good salad needs.

METHOD

1 **For the barbecue baby carrots**, cut the carrots in half lengthways. Cook in a ceramic-shelled, lidded barbecue at 200°C/400°F for 4 minutes, until charred.

2 **For the pickled baby carrots**, bring the sugar, vinegar, thyme, rosemary and bay leaf to the boil. Finely slice the carrots lengthways and pickle them in the mixture for a few hours.

3 **For the baby beetroot**, vacuum-pack each variety of beetroot in a separate bag, add butter, salt and pepper to each bag. Steam for 20 minutes and allow to cool.

4 **For the basil purée**, preheat the oven to 110°C/225°F/gas mark ¼. Twice-peel each courgette and vacuum-pack with the peelings and all the other ingredients. Steam in the oven for 15 minutes. Blitz for 1–2 minutes in blender. Put the basil purée back in the vac packs until needed.

5 **For the confit cherry tomatoes**, preheat the oven to 110°C/225°F/gas mark ¼. Blanch the tomatoes in boiling water and then refresh in ice-cold water. Remove the skins, halve the tomatoes and lay on a tray, flat-side-up. On each half tomato, place a garlic clove slice, a leaf of thyme, salt, pepper and one-eighth of the icing sugar, then drizzle with lemon juice and olive oil. Cook the tomatoes in the oven for 5–10 minutes.

6 **For the onion croutons**, brunoise the onion bread from frozen and drizzle with onion oil. Cook until golden, then place the onion bread on kitchen paper to drain.

7 **To serve**, on each plate arrange a barbecued carrot, a pickled carrot, 2 baby beetroot, 2 confit tomato halves and some onion croutons, along with the basil purée, to taste. Garnish with baby rocket, borage flowers, pea shoots, purple pea pods, cucumber flowers, redcurrants, mustard leaves and fennel.

SPRING ONION CALENDAR

PLANT To have a year-round supply, sow once in spring for harvesting from late summer and again in late summer or autumn to be ready from early summer the following year. Plant sets in spring in shallow drills and cover them so the necks are just protruding from the soil.
CARE Weed regularly and water sparingly.
HARVEST Crop spring onions as soon as the foliage starts to yellow.

SPRING ONIONS

Colin and Slawek grow spring onions and garlic together, alternating rows of each, which they believe helps to ward off problems with pests. They use a red spring onion variety, called 'Redmate'. Once germinated, they thin it out by harvesting as and when the produce is required for the restaurant.

18

SKYE GYNGELL AT HECKFIELD PLACE

Hampshire

Long before Heckfield Place reopened as a hotel and spa, the head gardener, Paul Goacher, and culinary director, Skye Gyngell, were planning the productive areas of this eighteenth-century, Georgian estate in Hampshire, with its own 162-hectare/400-acre farm. Skye drew up a wish list of her most beloved fruit and vegetables to establish with Paul, who was at RHS Garden Wisley for more than twenty years, what could and could not be grown. Crops such as the chef's favourite 'Ratte' potato were a must for Skye because of its superb flavour and texture, while certain heritage pea varieties she favoured proved hard to track down so alternatives had to be found. In the end the list included some six hundred varieties. As Skye had discovered when she was at the Petersham Nurseries Café, where she was awarded a Michelin star, it is vital to have close collaboration between chef and grower – to get crops that are exciting and will shape your menus as well as to ensure that you do not end up getting carried away and growing food you do not use.

Skye is reluctant to get drawn into the complicated argument about seasonal organic and local produce.

As a chef, Skye finds nature exquisite and beautiful and would find it too hard to deny herself some ingredients because they could not be grown within 8 kilometres/5 miles of her kitchen. She therefore cooks simple delicious food that is produce-driven and that tastes superb – this might be asparagus in late spring or blood oranges in early autumn. She believes in the Slow Food Movement, which grew out of Carlo Petrini's protest against the opening of a McDonald's restaurant in Piazza di Spagna, Rome in 1986. The movement celebrates regional produce and traditional foods, often grown organically. That said, sustainability, provenance and the passion of individual producers governs Skye's choice when it comes to buying in any ingredients that Paul is not able to grow in the Hampshire soil.

The soil at Heckfield Place is predominantly loamy soil over a band of clay on the surrounding farmland, which is prone to exposure during harsh weather. Its correct preparation, Paul believes, is fundamental to healthy bountiful crops. He and his staff therefore dig well-rotted organic matter into the legume bed and add lime to the brassica one, while in the walled garden they work manure into the entire site.

To produce enough crops for the hotel's three restaurants as well as one in central London, Paul utilized several sites in the hotel's grounds. Attractively colourful types of produce such as rainbow chard, French beans, borlotti beans, globe artichokes and chives thrive in the 0.4-hectare/1-acre walled garden. Meanwhile the 2-hectare/5-acre field, which was located five minutes down the track from the walled

The grower,
Paul Goacher

Culinary director,
Skye Gyngell

OPPOSITE The walled garden, designed by Todd Longstaffe-Gowan, features crops, such as artichokes and climbing beans, that add a decorative element to the planting scheme.

garden to the farmhouse, is cultivated in the typical style of the surrounding arable farmland – row upon row of uniformly-grown crops, grouped together by type. There, Paul implements a four-year rotation of brassicas, legumes, roots/alliums and potatoes. There is also a herb garden and a newly planted orchard with dessert and culinary apples, plums and pears, which increased the yield of the original mini-orchard at the back of the farmhouse.

Working out the correct amount of produce to grow is still a learning process. Before the hotel and restaurant opened, the harvests were used for recipe development and spoils for the hard-working staff so it was difficult to determine the future quantities needed for each crop. Paul and his team have kept meticulous records about what has and has not worked, noting down growing conditions and whether the kitchen liked each crop or not. In years to come both Paul and Skye are keen to conduct growing trials, testing twenty different varieties of

a crop to establish which ones are suitable for the growing conditions, taste the best and look good. They both like heritage varieties and feel they are worth growing because of their superior flavour, even though, in some cases, they may be prone to disease or produce a smaller yield. Skye is happy to celebrate a small bounty by making something as a one-off on the daily menu, letting her food become 'simpler and more produce-inspired, where flavours are more inclined to whisper than roar', as she says herself.

While the seventeen-strong gardening team are on hand to harvest the produce, Paul and Skye are keen that both chefs and gardeners spend time experiencing each other's roles to see the effort required to grow, prepare and create a dish. They feel strongly that each group should have a mutual respect for each other's job.

Skye is a great believer in the idea that there is always more to learn. She plans for example to broaden the reach of the hotel's food provenance, to include milling and making their own bread as well as producing unpasteurized milk, so the future looks busy at Heckfield Place.

BELOW LEFT Skye and Paul have plans to extend the old orchard and increase the yield of plums and apples.
BELOW RIGHT Paul checks the dwarf French beans growing in the fields at Heckfield Place.

PLUM CALENDAR

PLANT Before planting, in autumn, check whether the plum variety is self-fertile. If it is, it can be planted on its own; otherwise you will need to plant two plum trees so they can fertilize each other. Although plums prefer moisture-retentive soil, make sure it is free-draining.

CARE Thin fruit if the branches are liable to break under its weight. Water and feed with a nitrogen-based fertilizer or mulch with well-rotted farmyard manure in autumn.

HARVEST Harvest when the plums feel soft.

ROSE HIP CALENDAR

PLANT Plant bare-root roses in autumn with plenty of organic manure added to each planting hole, which should be twice the width of the roots and a spade blade's depth. Mulch around each plant. Container-grown roses can be planted at any time of year.

CARE Water well and do not let plants dry out. Apply slow-release fertilizer in spring.

HARVEST Leave the flowers to develop into hips, which can then be harvested from late summer into autumn.

PLUMS

At the back of the farmhouse Paul and Skye inherited an orchard filled with unnamed old trees. This inspired them to create a new, 1.25-hectare/3-acre orchard in a sunny site nearby, which Paul and his team planted with varieties of plum, pear and apple. They selected bush trees, to create an authentic country feel, rather than the commercial spindle types. Paul protects the delicate flowers from frosts and windy conditions using horticultural fleece.

ROSE HIPS

As it is a great source of vitamin C, Paul leaves the hedgehog rose (*Rosa rugosa*) in the ornamental walled garden to develop hips for the kitchen at Heckfield Place. He also manages this species in the farm hedgerows and has planted new hedges with it in the mix.

PLUM & ALMOND FLAN

SERVES 6

INGREDIENTS

SHORTCRUST PASTRY
250g/9oz plain flour
1 tbsp caster sugar
$^1/_2$ tsp vanilla extract
1 organic, free-range egg
125g/4oz chilled unsalted butter, cubed
2 tbsp cold water

ALMOND FILLING
300g/10oz shelled whole almonds
300g/10oz unsalted butter
300g/10oz caster sugar
6 organic, free-range egg yolks
Vanilla extract
Rind of 1 lemon

TO FINISH
10 plums

This is a lovely, not too sweet tart that works best when served with crème fraîche.

METHOD

1 **For the shortcrust pastry**, place the flour, sugar, vanilla extract, egg and butter in a food processor, blitz until you have a consistency of wet sand (you can also do this mixing by hand or in a food mixer with a hook attachment). Add the cold water and continue to process – the dough will come together into a smooth ball. Wrap the dough with clingfilm and chill for at least 30 minutes in the refrigerator.

2 **For the almond filling**, preheat the oven to 200°C/400°F/gas mark 6. Lay the almonds on a baking sheet and put in the oven for 3–4 minutes, to warm them and so tickle out the flavour. Remove and cool. Grind the almonds in a food processor until they are coarsely chopped. Add the butter and sugar, then continue processing. With the motor still running, add the egg yolks one at a time through the feed tube, then put in a few drops of vanilla extract. You should have a smooth paste by now. Stir in the lemon rind. The almond filling can be used right away, or chilled for later use.

3 **To finish the flan**, preheat the oven to 190°C/375°F/gas mark 5. Roll out the chilled pastry dough to a thickness of 2mm/$^1/_{16}$in and use it to line a flan tin, 25–26cm/10–10$^1/_2$in wide. Place some greaseproof paper or nonstick baking paper over the pastry dough and cover it with some uncooked beans, rice or pastry weights. Bake for 15–20 minutes. Remove the beans, rice or weights and paper from the pastry case, then spoon in the almond filling and smooth over. Chop the plums in half, remove the stones and place skin-side-up in the almond filling. Return the flan tin to the oven and cook for a further 30–45 minutes, until the surface is golden brown and firm to touch. Cover the flan loosely with tinfoil if it is browning too quickly. When done, remove and cool.

PAUL & SKYE'S
KITCHEN GARDEN SECRETS

- **Use cloches to extend the season**: In early spring warm the soil with cloches, in preparation for sowing seeds, and then again in autumn use them to prolong crop productivity.
- **Feed asparagus**: If you can find it, apply freshly gathered seaweed as a mulch around asparagus in mid- or late winter. If you cannot source seaweed, use manure as an alternative mulch.
- **Parsley in winter**: Cut parsley back at the end of the growing season and transplant into pots to go in the greenhouse or on a windowsill, or into a cold frame.
- **Spring pickup**: In autumn apply slow-release fertilizer such as bonemeal to fruit trees – both tree fruit and soft fruit varieties. This will give them a boost in spring.
- **Protect peaches**: Cover outdoor-grown peaches in late autumn with horticultural plastic film. This is more about keeping the trees dry rather than frost-free, so they do not develop the bacterial infection peach leaf curl, which develops in moist conditions.

ROSE HIP SYRUP

SERVES 10

It really is worth spending a little time picking rose hips and making this unusual elegant syrup, which is perfect with any soft creamy cheese.

METHOD

1   Wash the rose hips and remove their stalks. Pulse the hips in a food processor to chop coarsely. Quickly place the hip pieces in a saucepan of 175ml/6fl oz boiling water. Once the water has come back to the boil, remove the pan from the heat and let it stand for 15 minutes. Then strain, reserving the liquid. In another 175ml/6fl oz boiling water, repeat this boiling process and strain once more. Having strained off the liquid, this time discard the rose hips.

2   Measure the strained liquid, then put it back in the saucepan on the heat. For each 1 litre/1¾ pints of strained liquid add 750g/1½lb caster sugar. Stir to help dissolve the sugar. Once it has boiled and the sugar dissolved, remove from the heat and pour the syrup into sterilized jars to cool. Serve with dandelion leaves and Wigmore cheese.

INGREDIENTS

1kg/2lb 3oz rose hips
350ml/12fl oz water
750g/1½lb caster sugar

TO SERVE
Dandelion leaves
Wigmore cheese

19

WIMPOLE HALL

Cambridgeshire

For years, the majority of crops grown in the spectacular, 1.8-hectare/4½-acre walled garden at the National Trust's Wimpole Hall in Cambridgeshire was sold to visitors, because the kitchen preferred buying in timesaving, pre-prepared produce. In the last five years or so things have changed, both in response to new directives from the Trust and to renewed interest in produce among the chefs working in the café.

Among the advocates of this new approach are Philip Whaites, head gardener at Wimpole Hall for thirty-two years, and the Trust's development chef, Clive Goudercourt. Clive, who is responsible for developing recipes and menus that can be adopted by property teams, cafés and outlets throughout the National Trust, is passionate about cooking and believes it is an adventure that starts in the garden and needs the dedication and devotion of a gardener and his team. At Wimpole Hall, there are three full-time gardeners, including Philip, as well as a seasonal gardener and seventy volunteers who help to cultivate around 70 per cent of the produce used

in the café. Similarly the café kitchen has three staff, including head chef Adam Jennings.

In addition to assessing the size, colour, shape and flavour of each crop grown in the walled garden, he also takes great care to choose varieties that are suitable for the soil and conditions and perhaps, most importantly, does not water them too much. This helps crops develop a strong root system as they seek out the natural water source. Crops grown in this way have a more intense flavour and better texture

OPPOSITE The walled garden at Wimpole Hall is a traditional potager design, divided into four main quadrants.
BELOW Cut flowers are grown for the house and restaurant and introduce colour and interest throughout the year.

The grower,
Philip Whaites

The chef,
Clive Goudercourt

than shop-bought produce, and can also be kept for longer. Philip cites careful preparation of the loam over heavy clay soil as another reason why he and his team produce such delicious crops. In autumn they dig in home-made compost and chicken manure and then rake it to create a fine tilth. This helps crops such as carrots and parsnips, which would otherwise develop forked roots in the stony clay soil.

Wimpole is one of the National Trust's larger kitchen gardens. The garden is divided into four quadrants, with espaliered pears set in the centre. One quadrant is allotted to the volunteers, so they can showcase different crops and their growing techniques to inspire visitors. The remaining three quadrants are the productive garden and comprise root, legume and allium beds. The crops are moved around the beds on a four-year rotation system.

As visitors are the main focus at Wimpole Hall, anything that is grown has to tell a story that is engaging and informative, so it is not always possible to harvest a whole crop. Philip and Clive therefore

BELOW The walled garden is designed both to be productive and attractive to the many visitors.

find it difficult to assess the volume of crops required at any one time. The garden teams deal with this situation by just growing the crops they want and the kitchen uses as much as it can. In early spring they plant more than three hundred onion sets of both 'Red Baron' and 'Senshyu' as well as direct sow spring onions. They have grown kohl rabi from seed too, though on the dry soil at Wimpole Hall it is hard to get this going – kohl rabi prefers wetter conditions.

The combination of warm days and cold nights, which is typical of spring at Wimpole Hall, is not helpful when growing vegetables, but this does not deter Philip from growing pumpkins and squash, which have always been a favourite at Wimpole. Philip starts the pumpkins and squash in the greenhouse in late winter or early spring and hardens the young plants off before planting them in their final positions outside.

Philip grows a good range of root crops: for example 'Solar Yellow', 'Paris Market Atlas' and 'Flyaway' carrots; five types of beetroot – 'Boston', 'Chioggia', 'Burpees Golden', 'Detroit' and 'Boltardy'; and the quick-growing, hybrid parsnip 'Gladiator'. He believes beetroot in particular is vastly underused, even though its sweet earthy flavour should satisfy the British palate perfectly.

Philip is keen to encourage the chefs to try new types of vegetable and is currently growing 'Giant Prague' celeriac and bunching (rather than blanched) celery. Alongside the second early potato variety 'Kestrel', he has introduced a rare variety of maincrop potato, 'Stemster'. It is a great all-rounder, so useful for the kitchen, and is widely grown in France, but seldom grown in the UK – largely, Philip believes, because the red skin is too pale for supermarket tastes. However 'Stemster' is high-yielding, has good disease resistance and – crucially for East Anglia's dry climate – copes well in drought.

To remind the chefs where the produce comes from, Philip and Clive encourage them to plant, water and pick the crops. Clive also likes the chefs to vary the vegetable accompaniments daily, depending on what is available in the garden. There is always the opportunity to create a quick recipe from a small crop – it could be a few gooseberries, which could be made into a fruit crumble or fool.

PHILIP & CLIVE'S
KITCHEN GARDEN SECRETS

- **Reduce the risks of muscle strain or blisters**:
Gardening is a very healthy, physical activity, so always
choose your tools carefully so that you do not injure
yourself. Select a tool that feels right and is made by an
established manufacturer. Cheap tools can be unfit for
purpose and should generally be avoided.
- **Avoid compacting soil**: Consider creating no-dig
raised beds in your patch. Philip lays bark chips between
his beds to reduce compaction and create easy access
to the beds, even in the worst ground conditions. It
also improves the quality and quantity of vegetables
produced in a small space.
- **Select single (nectar-rich) flowers**: Plant these
near your vegetables so they attract beneficial insects not
just in the garden but in the wider environment.
- **Sow correct amounts of seed**: Always divide your
seeds up before sowing. If you apply them direct from the
packet, it is far too easy to make a mistake and oversow.
- **Get seeds off to a flying start**: Philip always waters
his seed drills before sowing, especially beetroot seeds.

PEAR CALENDAR

PLANT It is important to select the appropriate pear rootstock for the type of tree habit you want: 'Quince A' for espalier-trained or bare-root bush trees; and 'Quince C' for cordon varieties and pear trees grown in pots. Plant in autumn, in a sunny spot, and water during dry spells.
CARE Add a general fertilizer in spring, and prune according to the tree's shape.
HARVEST Pick pears before they are ripe and leave them in a cool dry store to develop.

PARSNIP CALENDAR

SOW Wait until early or mid-spring, when the soil has warmed slightly, to direct sow parsnips. Then place three seeds together at 15cm/6in intervals, 1cm/$\frac{1}{2}$in deep in rows 30cm/12in apart.
CARE When they are 2.5cm/1in tall, with true leaves, thin to one seedling at each point. Weed by hand and keep the soil well watered.
HARVEST Wait for a frost and the foliage to die back in autumn before lifting the crop carefully.

PEARS

In the centre of the walled garden at Wimpole Hall are pear trees grown on espalier frames. The varieties are 'Conference', 'Doyenné du Comice' and 'Beurré Hardy'. This year Philip found that some of the pear trees, which are twelve years old, were not cropping well, so he may replace them if they have another poor growing season. The alkaline chalky soil of the walled garden is not ideal for pears so the poor yield might also be a cumulative result of being deficient in some trace elements, though Philip does apply an appropriate feed throughout the year to address this. He is likely to plant any replacement trees on a different site.

Pears do not store well so the team leaves them in the apple store for only a week, while they ripen to perfection, before taking them to the kitchen. For small harvests Philip leaves the fruit on the tree and picks it over several weeks.

PARSNIPS

To extend the growing season at Wimpole Hall by producing early crops, Philip sows 'Gladiator' parsnips in nine modular trays in the polytunnel in early spring. When they have produced their first true leaves, in mid- and late spring, he hardens them off outdoors, initially covering the trays with horticultural fleece. His trick is to allow the parsnip seedlings to establish but not linger in the cells too long before transplanting, as this can damage their root systems if special care is not taken. Philip does direct sow outdoors too, but these crops will not be as big or as plentiful as those started off indoors earlier in the year. He feeds the beds in autumn with organic chicken manure from the estate, so when it comes to planting time it has broken down in the soil. Philip uses a 'rabbit' spade to harvest the parsnips, carefully edging down one side of the root to allow him to tease the parsnip out, intact and with a perfectly tapered root.

PEAR & SHORTBREAD CRUMBLE WITH LIME SORBET

SERVES 2

Autumn is also one of the most abundant times for crops. Pears lightly poached and served with shortbread and sorbet is one of those real indulgences at that time of year, especially in early autumn, when the weather is still mild. I think this dessert rounds off a heavy roast dinner perfectly – it is refreshing and light and will leave you savouring every last morsel. When finished with a buttery shortbread biscuit, this dish is absolutely wonderful.

METHOD

1   **For the citrus pear slices**, infuse the pear slices in the water with the lemon juice for about 15 minutes.

2   **For the red wine poached pear cubes**, place the pear cubes in a saucepan, add the wine and the sugar. Bring to the boil, then reduce the heat to a simmer and cook the pear cubes for 5 minutes, until soft. Remove from the pan and place to one side to cool. Continue boiling the wine until reduced and thick.

3   **For the pear 'boats'**, place the pear halves in a saucepan with the white wine, thyme, sugar, cinnamon and orange juice. Bring to the boil and then gently simmer for 20–30 minutes, or until a knife slips easily into the pear flesh.

4   **For the shortbread crumbs**, crush the shortbread biscuit and mix in the orange rind.

5   **To serve**, on each plate set a shortbread biscuit, followed by a pear 'boat', hollow side upwards. Fill the hollow with half the cubed pears. Then arrange half the sliced pears in a fan shape on each plate. Put a few of the shortbread crumbs on each plate and add a scoop of sorbet or ice cream on top of the crumbs, which will stop the sorbet sliding around. Sprinkle the remaining shortbread crumbs over the dessert and drizzle over the retained red wine syrup.

INGREDIENTS

CITRUS PEAR SLICES
$^{1}/_{2}$ pear, peeled, cored and thinly sliced
100ml/3$^{1}/_{2}$fl oz water
Juice of $^{1}/_{2}$ lemon

RED WINE POACHED PEAR CUBES
$^{1}/_{2}$ a pear, peeled, cored and thinly cubed
100ml/3$^{1}/_{2}$fl oz red wine
30g/1oz caster sugar

PEAR 'BOATS'
1 pear, peeled, cored and cut in half
100ml/3$^{1}/_{2}$fl oz white wine
A few thyme leaves
50g/2oz caster sugar
Cinnamon stick
Juice of 1 orange

SHORTBREAD CRUMBS
1 all-butter shortbread biscuit
Rind of 1 orange

TO SERVE
2 all-butter shortbread biscuits
Lime sorbet or ice cream

YORKSHIRE PUDDING WITH PURÉED PARSNIPS & ROASTED VEGETABLES

SERVES 4

INGREDIENTS

ROASTED VEGETABLES
2 parsnips, peeled and cut into batons
2 carrots, peeled and cut into batons
$^1/_4$ swede, peeled and cut into batons
2 sticks of celery, cut into batons
Red onion, cut into wedges
150g/5oz baby corn
2 tbsp extra-virgin cold-pressed
   rapeseed oil
Salt and pepper

CHILLI SAUCE
2 red chillies
50ml/2fl oz extra-virgin cold-pressed
   rapeseed oil
Juice of $^1/_2$ lime
Small handful of parsley, chopped

PARSNIP MASH
350g/12oz parsnips, peeled and
   roughly chopped
Good knob of unsalted butter
2 tbsp double cream
Salt and pepper

YORKSHIRE PUDDINGS
2 eggs
80g/2$^1/_2$oz plain flour
130ml/4$^1/_2$fl oz milk
Rapeseed oil, for coating the tin

CARAMELIZED ONIONS
50g/2oz butter
500g/1lb 1oz red onions, thinly sliced
Generous handful of thyme leaves
2 tbsp red wine vinegar
30g/1oz brown sugar

PURÉED LEEK
30g/1oz butter
Large leek, trimmed, cleaned and
   thinly sliced (include the green
   part as well as the white)
Salt and pepper

TO SERVE
Chopped mixed herbs, to garnish
100g/3$^1/_2$oz per person of rare
   roasted sirloin

Many people enjoy roast potatoes and Yorkshire pudding, but they may overlook parsnips as an alternative to potatoes, even though they are as versatile. Clive likes to use parsnips, and in this recipe he has mashed some of them and roasted others. As a mash, parsnip is rich and buttery with a smooth texture. When roasted, it has a rich flavour, which is enhanced if the parsnips slightly caramelize on the outside; when paired with a little honey, roast parsnips are glorious. You can even fry the peelings for parsnip crisps. The recipe Clive uses for Yorkshire puddings has equal quantities of the various ingredients, so use a cup or ramekin or similar and make sure all the ingredients fill the container to the rim. Another way is to crack the eggs into a measuring jug and note their volume. Use the same volume for the flour and milk. When roasting beef, Clive prefers sirloin, but you could use topside or silverside.

METHOD

1   **For the roasted vegetables**, preheat the oven to 180°C/350°F/gas mark 4. Place the vegetables in a roasting tin, drizzle over the oil and shake to coat. Sprinkle over a pinch of salt and pepper, and place in the oven for 15 minutes. Then give the roasting tin a shake to make sure the vegetables roast evenly and return to the oven until the vegetables are soft and lightly coloured.

2   **For the chilli sauce**, with a skewer, fork or tongs, hold the chillies over a flame to blacken the skins. Then place them in a small bowl and cover with clingfilm. After 5 minutes, remove the clingfilm, then peel the chillies. Cut the chillies in half and remove the seeds. Place the chillies in a blender and blitz into the oil. Then add lime juice and parsley.

3   **For the parsnip mash**, place the parsnips into a saucepan of water and boil for 15–20 minutes, until soft. Remove the saucepan from the heat and drain the parsnips, using a colander. Place the colander over the top of the saucepan and put to one side for 5 minutes, until the parsnips start to dry. Tip the parsnips in a bowl, add the butter and cream, and mash using a fork or potato masher. Parsnip mash needs to be slightly lumpy rather than perfectly smooth. Use salt and pepper to season, and then put the mash to one side.

4   **For the Yorkshire puddings**, preheat the oven to 220°C/425°F/gas mark 7. Place the eggs, flour and milk in a bowl and mix with a stick

blender or whisk until combined and smooth. Place a little oil in each hole in a mini-muffin tin and put into the oven. When it is smoking hot, open the oven door and quickly pour the batter into each of the holes until they are half full. Shut the door and cook for 15–20 minutes, until risen and golden. Once the batter has risen, remove the Yorkshire puddings from the oven and loosen each one from its hole. Turn them upside down and return to the oven for 2 minutes, to crisp the bottoms.

5 **For the caramelized onions**, melt the butter in a heavy-based saucepan. Add the onions and thyme and sauté gently for 2 minutes, until softening. Add the remaining ingredients and stir well. Cover the saucepan with a lid, lower the heat and allow to cook gently for about 30 minutes. Stir occasionally. Remove the lid, increase the heat and stir quickly for 2 minutes, or until the liquid thickens and reduces.

6 **For the puréed leek**, place the butter in a saucepan and add the sliced leek. Cover the saucepan while the leek sautées until soft, about 5 minutes. Remove from the heat and use a stick blender to blitz to a purée. Add salt and pepper, to taste.

7 **To serve**, make sure everything is piping hot – reheat as you need. Place a spoonful of the parsnip mash on each plate and arrange some roast parsnip batons around this in the style of a tepee – this gives height and makes the parsnips the main focus. Place a portion of the other roasted vegetables on the plate and garnish with a few chopped herbs. Swoosh the leek purée around the plate. Put a Yorkshire pudding on the plate and fill with the caramelized onions, top with the rare roast beef and then finish with a drizzle of chilli sauce.

20

LE MANOIR
AUX QUAT'SAISONS

Oxfordshire

Raymond Blanc has played a huge part in reconnecting food-lovers with the idea of food provenance and seasonality. Thirty years ago, when nobody in Britain acknowledged or seemed to care how superior home-grown produce tasted when compared with commercially-grown produce, Raymond Blanc was devising how to grow his own vegetables for use in the kitchens of his new Oxfordshire hotel and restaurant, Le Manoir aux Quat'Saisons. In this he was way ahead of his time, and his ground-breaking vision had far-reaching effects and still inspires some of our most exciting, modern-day chefs.

Today Le Manoir's 0.8-hectare/2-acre, 100 per cent organic vegetable garden is something of a mecca for aspiring chefs and growers alike, who celebrate both its culinary and horticultural excellence. More than ninety varieties of vegetables, more than seventy varieties of herbs and twenty different edible mushrooms are produced there each year. During the growing season that means the garden supplies 70 per cent of the herbs and 13 per cent of the vegetables used in the kitchen – impressive figures when you consider forty chefs create 72,000 delectable plates of food each year.

The vegetable garden fills a beautiful space on a north-east slope at Le Manoir. Shelter is provided by eighty-year-old oaks and willows, and a Cotswold stone wall forms the dividing boundary between this productive area and the formal lawns and lavender-lined stone paths. Overseen by head gardener Anne-Marie Owens and eight other full-time staff, the vegetable garden is exquisite – a masterclass of order and impeccable standards where even green manures are grown in orderly rows. Far from being 'behind the scenes' the produce garden is open to hotel guests and group tours, yet it is also a vital working element of Le Manoir. The garden is

OPPOSITE Anne-Marie Owens has worked with Raymond Blanc for more than twenty years in Le Manoir's 11 hectares/27 acres of kitchen and ornamental gardens.
BELOW The magnificent gardens at Le Manoir are tended by Anne-Marie and her team of eight gardeners.

The grower,
Anne-Marie Owens

The chef,
Raymond Blanc

part trial ground (where between twenty and fifty varieties of a single vegetable will be cultivated) and part laboratory (where chefs and gardeners taste and analyse the flavour and texture of each variety to see which, if any, will make it on to the menu). Every two weeks Raymond and Anne-Marie, together with head chef Gary Jones, sit down and discuss the different varieties of each vegetable they have grown in the trials that season. Their sole preoccupation is with the best-tasting varieties.

Early every morning, armed with the chefs' picking list for the day's lunch and dinner service, the gardening team start the time-consuming job of selecting and harvesting the appropriate crops so the chefs in the kitchen can wash and prepare them.

Once crops have been harvested and the beds are not required for a time, Anne-Marie likes to sow a green manure to feed the soil and help to improve its structure. For this she chooses phacelia, mustard and raddish seeds as they are quick growing. In mid-

autumn, she and her team also sow field beans to fix nitrogen into the soil; when this crop reaches 45cm/18in tall it is cut down and dug into the soil. The beds are netted to protect them from hungry muntjac deer.

BLOOMING COURGETTES

One of Raymond's signature dishes is a courgette flower stuffed with fresh peas and mint. It is the centrepiece of the charmingly named dish, 'Assiette Anne-Marie', that Raymond created for his gardening guru. Being delicate, seasonal and a burst of colour on the plate, 'Assiette Anne-Marie' is a feast for the eyes and palate. At Le Manoir they grow their own courgette flowers as they are best when eaten within hours of being picked; harvesting and transporting such flowers are notoriously tricky, which makes them hard to buy – and expensive too. The kitchen uses two hundred flowers a day throughout the summer months to create 'Assiette Anne-Marie', so there is

BELOW The garden team use cloches to extend the growing season and protect the crops from pests.

plenty of pressure for Anne-Marie and her team to produce consistent quantities of pristine blooms.

The courgette variety grown at Le Manoir is 'Nero di Milano', chosen primarily for its large flowers. Interestingly, seed companies emphasize its Italian heritage as opposed to its yield or uniformity. The garden team combat these potential shortcomings by ensuring that, after each growing season, the soil is well fed and nutrients replaced in the 30m/100ft polytunnel dedicated to courgettes.

To meet the daily demand for the courgette flowers, the team sow successively. Harvesting the flowers is done by hand each morning, and the daily scene of two gardeners each pushing a wheelbarrow-load of blue crates carefully filled with large open courgette blooms from the polytunnel through the garden to the kitchen door is a memorable sight. As both the male and female flowers are picked, there is no bountiful supply of courgette fruits and only a small percentage of them makes it into the kitchen.

BELOW While it is crucial that the vegetable borders are as productive as possible, care and attention are paid to their presentation and design too.

ABOVE During summer, around 200 courgette flowers are used in the kitchens at Le Manoir every day.
BELOW Chefs are encouraged to work in the gardens and harvest herbs and crops.

EDIBLE FLOWERS

Courgette blooms are Le Manoir's signature edible flower. Broad beans and red runner beans are two other sacrifical veg crops that are set aside to provide the kitchen with flowers, as opposed to fruit. Pot marigolds, chicory, salad rocket, radish and borage are sown successively from late winter to early summer, such is the popularity of their flowers too. Thyme, sage, chives and wild garlic are also grown for the intense flavour of their flowers, which are used in only small quantities as they often introduce a strong taste to a dish. Chervil, bergamot and coriander are harvested once for their leaves, while the second flush of growth is left to bolt and flower.

Edible flowers are picked in the morning when they are full of moisture and then placed on a layer of newspaper to help keep them intact. They are stored in a cool room until needed.

MICRO-LEAVES

Le Manoir grows an array of micro-leaves in the polytunnel all year round, changing the varieties to suit the seasons and meet the kitchen's requirements. Once again the staff have been in the forefront of fashion, having cultivated micro-leaves for fifteen years. Their produce of young leaves ranges from mustards 'Red Giant', 'Green in Snow' and 'Ruby Streaks' to beetroot, dill, coriander, celery leaf, sorrel, watercress, amaranth, perilla, ice lettuce and red cabbage.

It has taken considerable trial and error to determine the best varieties for flavour and texture – the micro-leaves need to stay intact when they are combined with a dressing – and to establish the optimum time to harvest.

ABOVE A wide variety of micro-leaves are grown in polytunnels at Le Manoir.
BELOW Raymond Blanc uses micro-leaves to add a burst of flavour to a dish.

ANNE-MARIE & RAYMOND'S
KITCHEN GARDEN SECRETS

- **Choosing a variety**: Look out for specialist vegetable days held by nurseries around the country. They often provide tastings of different varieties.
- **Tomatoes**: Raymond's favourite tomato varieties are 'Roma', 'Marmande', 'Costoluto Fiorentino', 'Coeur De Boeuf' and 'San Marzano'. Anne-Marie gives them as much space as possible as this really helps develop a healthy bushy plant as opposed to a leggy specimen. She supports plants with canes and pinches out the growing tip of each plant when it reaches 1.75m/6ft tall. To aid pollination, she taps the plants when in flower.
- **Successional sowing**: Sow spinach and radish every ten days or so from mid-spring to midsummer. Replace summer radishes with the winter variety from then onwards.
- **Grow through mulch**: Plant pumpkins and squash through black mulch matting to conserve moisture, prevent weeds and keep the fruit clean and intact.
- **Two is company**: Dill is planted next to brassicas and left to flower and so attract hoverflies. Geraniums (*Pelargonium*) too attract beneficial insects, while nasturtium (*Tropaeolum majus*) is grown alongside pumpkins and squash.

ASSIETTE ANNE-MARIE

SERVES 4

This is a true 'garden to plate' dish, and very simple to create. It emphasizes the values Raymond Blanc's mother and father instilled in him from an early age: respecting the land and its own ecosystem; looking forwards to the seasons; and cooking the food simply. This dish celebrates the very best that a garden has to offer.

METHOD

1   **For the stuffed courgette flowers**, in a small bowl, mix together the crushed peas, mint, salt, pepper and olive oil. Taste, correct the seasoning and put some stuffing inside each courgette flower. Place on a steamer tray or in a colander over a pan of boiling water covered with a lid, and steam for 8 minutes.

2   **To serve**, in a medium-sized saucepan on a high heat, bring the water, butter and salt to the boil. Add all the vegetables, cover with a lid and simmer for 3 minutes, until tender, then stir in the chervil. Place a hot stuffed courgette flower in one corner of each plate and fan out the baby courgettes in the opposite corner. Spoon the remaining vegetables around the plate and garnish with the pea shoots.

INGREDIENTS

STUFFED COURGETTE FLOWERS
120g/4oz garden peas, blanched, refreshed and crushed
Sprig of mint, chopped
2 pinches of sea salt
Pinch of pepper
2 tbsp extra-virgin olive oil
4 whole courgette flowers, stigmas and stamens removed

TO SERVE
75ml/2½fl oz water
25g/1oz butter
Pinch of sea salt
2 baby courgettes, cut into 1cm/½in pieces
8 green asparagus spears, cut into quarters
8 baby carrots, sliced
12 florets of purple sprouting broccoli
30g/1oz broad beans
10g/⅓oz garden peas
½ small bunch of fresh chervil, finely chopped
12 sprigs of pea shoots, to garnish

CONTACT DETAILS

In alphabetical order, running order in brackets and page reference in italics.

L'ENCLUME (**5**) *page 46*
Cavendish Street, Cartmel, Cumbria
LA11 6PZ
01539 536362
www.lenclume.co.uk

JACK STEIN (**4**) *page 38*
The Seafood Restaurant, Riverside,
Padstow, Cornwall PL28 8BY
01841 532700
www.rickstein.com

JEKKA'S HERBETUM (**10**) *page 92*
Rose Cottage, Shellards Lane,
Alveston, Gloucestershire
BS35 3SY
01454 418878
www.jekkasherbfarm.com

**LE MANOIR AUX
QUAT'SAISONS** (**20**) *page 178*
Church Road, Great Milton,
Oxfordshire OX44 7PD
01844 278881
www.manoir.com

MONACHYLE MHOR HOTEL
(**12**) *page 110*
Balquhidder, Lochearnhead,
Perthshire FK19 8PQ
01877 384622
http://mhor.net

PADSTOW KITCHEN GARDEN
(**4**) *page 38*
Trerethern Farm, Padstow,
Cornwall PL28 8LE
07974 697191
www.padstowkitchengarden.co.uk

RIVER COTTAGE (**9**) *page 84*
Park Farm, Trinity Hill Rd,
Axminster, Devon EX13 8TB
01297 630300
www.rivercottage.net

**SIR TERENCE CONRAN &
THE ALBION** (**15**) *page 134*
2–4 Boundary Street, Shoreditch,
London E2 7DD
020 7729 1051
www.albioncaff.co.uk

**SKYE GYNGELL AT
HECKFIELD PLACE**
(**18**) *page 162*
Heckfield, Hook, Hampshire
RG27 0LD
01189 326868
www.heckfieldplace.com

THE COMPANY OF COOKS
(**10**) *page 92*
The Old Kitchen, Kenwood
House, Hampstead Lane, London
NW3 7JR
020 8341 5384
www.companyofcooks.com

THE ETHICUREAN (**2**) *page 20*
Barley Wood Walled Garden,
Long Lane, Wrington, Somerset
BS40 5SA
01934 863713
www.ethicurean.com

THE FELIN FACH GRIFFIN
(**6**) *page 56*
Felin Fach, Brecon, Powys
LD3 0UB
01874 620111
www.felinfachgriffin.co.uk

THE GEORGE & DRAGON
(**3**) *page 30*
Clifton, Penrith, Cumbria
CA10 2ER
01768 865381
www.georgeanddragonclifton.
co.uk

THE GROVE (**1**) *page 10*
Molleston, Narberth,
Pembrokeshire SA67 8BX
01834 860915
www.thegrove-narberth.co.uk

THE PIG HOTEL (**7**) *page 66*
Beaulieu Road, Brockenhurst,
Hampshire SO42 7QL
01590 622354
www.thepighotel.com

THE RIVER CAFÉ (**11**) *page 102*
Thames Wharf, Rainville Road,
London W6 9HA
020 7386 4200
www.rivercafe.co.uk

**THE SCOTTISH KITCHEN
GARDEN** (**14**) *page 126*
The Scottish Café & Restaurant at The
Scottish National Gallery, The Mound,
Edinburgh EH2 2EL
0131 226 6524
www.thescottishcafeandrestaurant.com

THE STAR INN (**8**) *page 74*
Harome, Helmsley, North Yorkshire
YO62 5JE
01439 770397
www.thestaratharome.co.uk

THE WELLINGTON ARMS
(**16**) *page 144*
Baughurst Rd, Baughurst, Hampshire
RG26 5LP
01189 820110
www.thewellingtonarms.com

VALLUM FARM (**13**) *page 118*
Military Road, East Wallhouses,
Newcastle upon Tyne NE18 0LL
01434 672406
www.vallumfarm.co.uk

WIMPOLE HALL (**19**) *page 170*
Arrington, Royston, Cambridgeshire
SG8 0BW
01223 206000
www.nationaltrust.org.uk/
wimpole-estate

WINTERINGHAM FIELDS
(**17**) *page 154*
1 Silver St, Winteringham, Scunthorpe,
Lincolnshire DN15 9ND
01724 733096
www.winteringhamfields.co.uk

INDEX

Main recipe ingredients only are indexed. Page numbers in *italics* indicate an illustration; page numbers in **bold** indicate a main section on a particular vegetable.

ACKNOWLEDGMENTS

—◄━━━━►—

To the chefs, growers and behind-the-scenes-organizers who were involved with our book, thank you does not quite seem enough. But thank you, so much.

Thank you Helen, Becky and Joanna at Frances Lincoln – I think the word that springs to mind is 'patience'.

Mum and Dad, as always, thank you for being utterly amazing.

Carole and Bob, thank you for coming to the rescue when it came to yet another road trip.

Tory and Chef Paul Collins, Ava and George – thank you for introducing me to the delights of truly delicious food in the first place.

Syd, for keeping me company in my eyrie, and little Teddy for keeping my lap warm during the last few days of the edit.

To my darling Hal – thank you for waiting so beautifully until I finished on the 'pooter' so you could play Swashbuckle.

And to my darling Jason – not quite the romantic trip around the UK we first planned, but the most lovely, memorable journey to take with you nonetheless. We did it!

Cinead

Neither of us really knew how big a part of our lives this book was going to be, so I thank all our family and friends (to whom we owe so many suppers) for being so patient.

Mum and Dad, thank you for stepping in whenever we needed to head off on a shoot.

Val and Bernie, thank you for your continual support and grandparenting duties, without you guys this book would not have been possible.

Hal, son, thank you for having such an inquisitive mind and asking so many questions about what your Mummy and Daddy do for a job – one day it will all make sense.

Of course the stars of the show have been all the gardeners and chefs, whom I would like to thank all personally if only I had the room. You have made this book very special and opened our eyes to many new and wonderful ways to grow, cook and eat, thank you.

I would especially like to thank my good friend Jo Campbell, who has taught me so much about the art of veg growing; your dedication and knowledge are remarkable.

To my good friends at Le Manoir and The Ethicurean, where the seed of this project was sown, I had such a good couple of years working with you all.

Thank you to all the team at Frances Lincoln – Helen, Becky, Joanna and Sarah – for listening and being so patient with us. We got there in the end.

Antony, you have worked so hard editing the images for this book. I know it has been quite a journey, but I really appreciate it.

Darling Cinead, thank you so much for making our vision a reality. Creating this book together in eight months has been nothing short of a miracle – I have loved every minute of it. We have had quite a journey, but hopefully it will be one of many.

Jason